LORETTE WILMOT LIBRARY
Nazareth College of Rochester

Rochester City Ballet

Library of Congress Cataloging in Publication Data
Wentink, Andrew Mark.
Balletomania!
"A Gross Associates book."
1. Ballet—Miscellanea.   I. Title.
GV1787.W42   792.8
ISBN: 0–385–15072–5
Library of Congress Catalog Card Number 79–7611
Book Design by Beverley Gallegos

For Ruth, George, Paul, Dorothy, Lacy, Rita
and Henry—my colleagues and friends

Acknowledgments

For their help in compiling this book, I would like to thank: Miss Genevieve Oswald and her tireless staff at the Dance Collection, Performing Arts Research Center, The New York Public Library at Lincoln Center, for making such a wealth of dance information available to every serious dance lover; Walter Terry and Mr. and Mrs. A. J. Pischl, for allowing me to reproduce historical materials from their private collections; Frank Derbas, for all his ready and willing reproduction of historical materials; Martha Swope, Steven Caras, Fred Fehl, Beverley Gallegos, Edward Griffiths, Mydstkov, and Anthony Crickmay, for their photographs; Harold Kuebler and Joseph Gonzalez, of Doubleday & Company, for their enthusiasm for this project; Bill and Andrea Thompson and Arlene Gross, for their belief in the book; and, most of all, Jerry Gross, who conceived of this project in the first place, for his ideas, his encouragement, and his friendship throughout.

Contents

Foreword
by Patricia McBride

When I first traveled to Europe and Russia with the New York City Ballet in 1962, and danced in the beautiful theatres and opera houses of the European capitals, I was awed by the sense of ballet history and the memories of the great ballerinas that still lingered within those walls. Dancing in those grand theatres where the legendary Camargo, Sallé, Taglioni, Elssler, Cerrito, Grisi, and Grahn had danced, gave me a sense of a glorious tradition, and more than ever, I wanted to learn more about it. Of course, I experienced the finest results of that long tradition by being able to work with George Balanchine, Jerome Robbins, and the wonderful dancers of the New York City Ballet, but there was little time to learn more about other dancers, other companies, and all the history that preceded us. Gradually, over the years, by listening to the stories of older dancers, by reading, and by more travel, I have discovered at least some of what I wanted to know about ballet history. I think a book such as *Balletomania* is a marvelous way to find out just how much information we have picked up over the years, and have a lot of fun doing it! Since dance disappears the moment after it is performed, events and performances become history faster than in any other art. So, there are many people I have danced with and many performances that I have given that are already part of that history—I hope every reader of this book has as much fun testing his memory about those events as I do in remembering them!

New York, 1979

Introduction

As with all the performing arts, the enjoyment of ballet lies, first and foremost, in experiencing the excitement of a performance. But the fact that the immediate thrill of ballet—beautifully trained bodies moving harmoniously in an endless variety of forms, expressing the total range of human emotion and imagination—is complete in itself does not diminish the pleasure that can be derived from exploring the history of ballet and the breadth of its artistic dimensions.

Ballet is the oldest form of theatrical dance in the Western world, stemming from even earlier folk and court dance forms. In its almost four hundred years of existence, ballet has inspired some of the world's greatest musicians, writers, and artists to contribute to its production and performance. Over those centuries, the center of the ballet world has shifted from France, to Italy, to Russia, and, in the last forty years, to the United States. Over the past two decades, ballet audiences have grown astronomically. Today, everyone, it seems, wants to see the ballet!

Followers of all the performing arts usually advance from one stage of understanding and involvement to another. There is the initial exposure to the art, when all is instant response: likes and dislikes are clearly delineated and uncomplicated. After further acquaintance, the devotee becomes more aware of the range of expression and form, and begins to experiment indiscriminately. Finally, after passing through the first two stages, he begins to develop discriminating taste in all forms of the art, judging each performance on its artistic merits, weighing the contribution of form and structure (choreography, in the case of ballet), lighting, costume and set design, technical execution and artistic interpretation. Having reached this level, our aficionado anticipates each performance as a gourmet approaches a delectable meal.

But just as one can't eat continually, attending performances nonstop is impossible. Despite the growing number of quality television programs such as "Dance in America," "Live from Lincoln Center," and the seasonal telecasts of *The Nutcracker,* it remains a fact that ballet cannot be brought directly into the home. Undaunted, ballet lovers, scholars, students, balletomanes, and neophyte fans love to gather together outside the theater and share facts, figures, and unusual anecdotes of their favorite art form.

This book is intended as a companion, a stimulus, to those ballet conversations. In it, I have attempted to gather a portion of the multitude of facts, figures, and stories that make ballet so unique and fascinating. *Balletomania* will, I hope, serve as a source of pleasant diversion and useful information for all ballet lovers, no matter what their level of involvement.

The quizzes, varied in format as well as in degree of difficulty, were chosen for their inherent interest, information, curiosity, and surprise. In compiling these questions, I became more aware than ever of how esoteric ballet can be, but also how much fun can be had in finding out all the lesser-known facts about an art that was once considered elite, but that is now growing by leaps and bounds, so to speak. Frequently, "easier" quizzes are immediately followed by more difficult questions in an effort to lead the reader to a deeper knowledge of the ballet. The "Who Am I?" "Name That Ballet," and "Who Said It?" quizzes might be for the more knowledgeable ballet lover, but they were designed to present their information in an anecdotal, amusing, or interesting way that will make the newcomer want to learn more. Most of the contemporary questions focus on ballet in the United States, for obvious reasons; but the general coverage, especially in the earlier, historical questions, is international in scope.

After years of studying dance, befriending dancers, and serving as a researcher, archivist, editor, and writer in the field, I decided to compile a book that would allow me to share some of the joy and fascination I have always found in the ballet. In response to the surprise of friends in hearing an unfamiliar piece of dance information, I have often found myself saying, "But I thought everyone knew that!" Well, everyone doesn't know all the wonderful things there are to know about ballet; I certainly don't! So, not only has this been a great opportunity for me to learn more about the dance, but it is my hope that readers will help me continue the process by submitting their own favorite facts, puzzles, anecdotes, and critical comments, in view of a possible sequel. For the information contained in this volume represents only a fraction of what there is to know and love in the world of ballet. And, as I have learned in the course of compiling this book, sharing our ballet knowledge can be *almost* as much fun, in its way, as being present at the ballet itself!

Andrew Mark Wentink
New York, 1979

The Quizzes

B

[1]

The ballet superstar of the 1970s is undoubtedly
Russian-born Mikhail Baryshnikov, for whose special tal-
ents many choreographers have wanted to create ballets.
Here he is seen in five of those new works.

I   Identify the ballets.

II Name the choreographer of each of these
    ballets.

17

C

D

MARTHA SWOPE PHOTOS

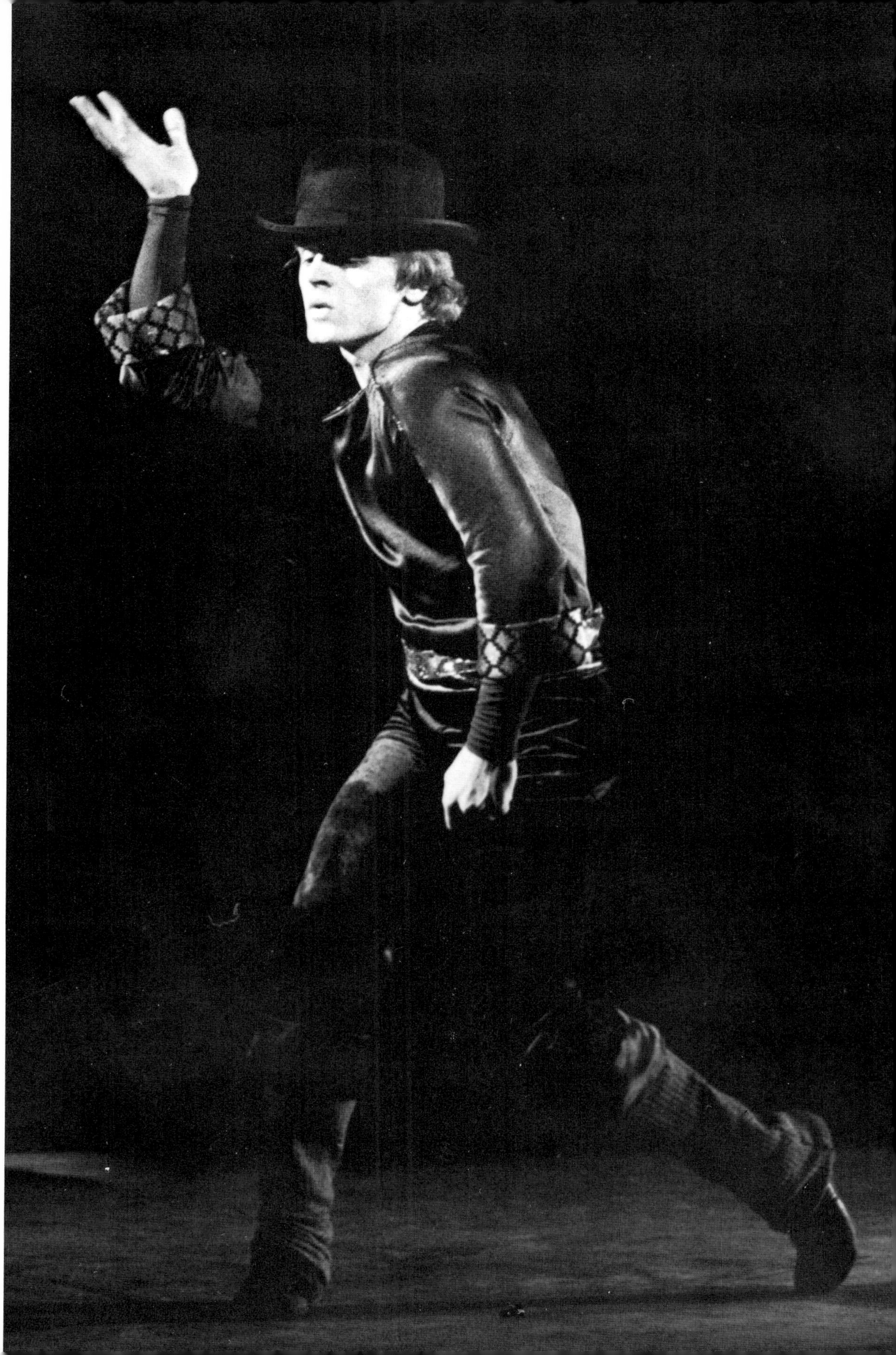

E

[2] WHO AM I?

IN the history of dance, I am known for raising my skirt above the ankle, jumping high, and perhaps inventing ballet steps of new virtuosity, such as the *entrechat*. My mentor, Mme. Prévost, grew so jealous of my popularity and success with the public, critics and her lover, M. Blondi, that she had me moved to the back line of the corps de ballet at the Paris Opera. But, when M. Dumoulin failed to show up for his solo in the demon dance, I ran from my place and improvised a dance that was hailed as a triumph. Fashions, desserts, and social dances were named after me, and, in 1930, a British society established to promote new ballets bore my name. I was born in Brussels in 1710, and though my real name was Marie-Anne de Cupis, soon after my 1726 success in Paris, I adopted the name of my Spanish grandmother.

Who am I?

[3] BALLET STEPS

SHOWN opposite is one of the foremost ballerinas of our time in a basic ballet positon.

   I What ballet step is she demonstrating?

   II Who is she?

[4] WHO SAID IT?

BELOW are four pithy remarks on dancing. Can you name the people to whom they are attributed?

(A) "To those of us with real understanding, dancing is the only pure art form!"

(B) "Ballet is woman."

(C) "Contrary to popular belief, choreography is the oldest profession."

(D) "The true, the unique, the eternal subject of a ballet is dancing."

SON

FATHER

[5] WHO AM I?

NOT inappropriately, I was called Le Dieu de la Danse (The God of the Dance) throughout most of my long and tumultuous career with the Paris Opera. The critics and public alike adored me for my extraordinary gifts of grace, elegance, and purity of style. It is no wonder that, when some foolish woman stepped on my foot, I had to tell her that she had put all of Paris into mourning for two weeks! There were rumors that, regardless of my great talent as a dancer, I was rather arrogant, boorish, and tasteless, and that when I was involved in choreographing, even the girls of the corps de ballet would laugh behind my back! All jealous, spiteful rumors, you can be sure! Like the other members of my large family of Italian singers and dancers, I was not bound by conventional morality; in fact, my longtime mistress, Marie Allard, bore me a son, whom you see pictured alongside me here. Of all the dancers of my time, he was the only one who could be considered greater than myself (naturally, he had *me* for a father!). His most special gift was perhaps his extremely high jump that caused two of his astounded admirers to have the following exchange: "How light he is! He must live on a diet of butterflies!" said one. "No," answered the other, "he eats only their wings."

   I Who am I?

  II What is my son's name?

THE first production that resembled a ballet as we know it today was commissioned by Catherine de Médicis, Queen of France, to celebrate the betrothal of her sister Marguerite de Lorraine to the Duc de Joyeuse, and was presented for the first time on October 15, 1581. Balthazar de Beaujoyeulx created the five-and-one-half-hour (!) spectacle that had as its theme the legend of Circe. However, more than a century earlier, in 1459, a precursor to this spectacle ballet had been presented by Bergonzio di Botta on the occasion of the wedding of the Duke of Milan and Isabella of Aragon. The ballet took place at the wedding banquet itself, where each course was served by figures impersonating Jason and the Argonauts; in the background, ensemble dances representing the dishes being served were performed. Later on in this lavish feast came a ballet based on the theme of conjugal bliss, followed by a grand bacchanale as a finale—and from here it only took five hundred years to get to Agon!

[6]

THIS costume design for a princess is by _____.

    a   Alexandre Benois

    b   Léon Bakst

    c   Louis Bouquet

    d   Oliver Messel

    e   Eugene Berman

THIS is the famous opening scene from a great Romantic ballet.

I   What is the title of the ballet?

II   Who choreographed the original production?

III   In what year and where was it first performed?

IV   What choreographer's version is accepted today on an equal plane with the original version?

V   Can you name the four couples seen here and on the following page in their interpretations of the principal roles?

MATCH these choreographers with the ballet classics they created and the ballerinas who first danced the title roles.

1	Arthur Saint-Léon	A	*Giselle*
2	Jean Dauberval	B	*Swan Lake*
3	Jules Perrot/Jean Coralli	C	*Sleeping Beauty*
4	Marius Petipa	D	*Coppélia*
5	Lev Ivanov/M. Petipa	E	*La Fille Mal Gardée*

a	Mlle. Theodore
b	Giuseppina Bozacchi
c	Pierina Legnani
d	Carlotta Brianza
e	Carlotta Grisi

[9]

MATCH these full-length classical ballets with their composers.

1	*Raymonda*	a	Leo Delibes
2	*Don Quixote*	b	Ludwig Minkus
3	*Harlequinade*	c	Alexander Glazounov
4	*Esmeralda*	d	Cesare Pugni
5	*Sylvia*	e	Riccardo Drigo

THIS title page and plate from a nineteenth-century book are rather irreverent depictions of the ballet *Flore et Zéphire.* The artist, "Theophile Wagstaff," is known for his great novels, which he illustrated himself.

Who is Theophile Wagstaff?

[11] WHO AM I?

I was considered quite early in my career the only serious rival to Mme. Taglioni, the reigning queen of the ballet. I did not dance with her pure, classic style, but my personality, which audiences found vivacious and even seductive, was received with equal enthusiasm. My solo dance from *Le Diable Boiteux,* which you see in figure (A), was an unmitigated triumph and established my reputation as the unrivaled interpreter of colorful national dances. After great successes in Vienna, Berlin, London, and Paris, I took my repertoire, highlighted by *Le Diable Boiteux* and the two other national dances shown in figures (B) and (C) on the following pages, to America. The day I appeared at a New York theater, May 14, 1840, I not only saved it from bankruptcy, I started a dance rage. The Congress of the United States of America adjourned to see me when I appeared in Washington, D.C., and some enthusiastic gentlemen in Baltimore unhitched the horses from my carriage and pulled it to my hotel establishment themselves! The revered American writer Ralph Waldo Emerson and his companion, Miss Fuller, attended one of my Boston performances. She said, "Ralph, this is poetry." He answered, "No, Margaret, it is religion!" I don't think anyone ever had a nicer compliment. Finally, after two years, I left America to continue dancing in the capitals of Europe (all except Paris, where I was banned because of an alleged breach-of-contract resulting from my American stay), until my retirement. When my career was over, I settled in my native Vienna, where I died in 1884.

    I   Who am I?

    II   What is the name of my most famous solo from *Le Diable Boiteux* (A)?

    III   What are the names of my other famous solos seen in (B) & (C)?

    IV   What was the name of the New York theater in which I made my American debut?

[12] PARTNERS ON AND OFF–STAGE

PICTURED opposite are two great names of nine-teenth-century ballet who also happened to be husband and wife.

    I   Who are they?

    II   For which ballet is he best known?

    III   Can you name the ballet they are danc-ing?

THE premiere of Nijinsky's ballet to Stravinsky's Le Sacre du Printemps (The Rite of Spring) *was one of the most important events in the history of twentieth-century music and ballet. From all written reports, it resulted in a scene of pandemonium that has rarely been equaled. While the dancers in the ballet were trying to perform Nijinsky's difficult and unfamiliar choreography, to Stravinsky's equally difficult and unfamiliar score, conducted by a very calm Pierre Monteux, the entire audience went berserk. People hooted and whistled and screamed. Half the audience was for it and half against. People got so carried away, they beat out time on their neighbors' heads, ladies slapped young men in the face, men challenged each other to duels, a grand countess stood up with her tiara awry and her face beet-red and shouted at the audience. Diaghilev stood in the wings, telling the stagehands to turn the house lights on and off, to calm the audience down. Nijinsky stood in the wings pounding out time with his feet and shouting out counts to the dancers that didn't even exist in the score. In a rage, Stravinsky stood, faced the audience and yelled "Go to Hell!" Police were called in to eject the more rowdy demonstrators. After the performance that evening, Diaghilev, Stravinsky, and Nijinsky sat in a restaurant rumi-nating on the fiasco that had occurred that evening. Thinking about the enormous publicity value of the* scandale, *Diaghilev said, "Exactly what I wanted."*

[13] WHO AM I?

THOUGH some called me "ugly as sin," my dancing was considered the finest male dancing of my generation. In fact, it was said that I gave dignity to male ballet dancing when the art was dominated by the great romantic ballerinas, Taglioni, Elssler, Grisi, Grahn, and Cerrito. I partnered and choreographed for all of them, sometimes for two, three, or even four of them in the same ballet! I worked in every dance capital in Europe, it seems, and was the most important influence on Russian ballet in St. Petersburg until the advent of Marius Petipa. I am seen here with the ballerina who was probably my greatest discovery. She has often been called my wife, but we actually never married. I did marry a ballerina, but a rather obscure one. One of my greatest disappointments was not to have choreographed the full ballet that made my mistress and protégée a star, but I did at least choreograph her solos!

I   Who am I?

II   Who is my partner, protégée and mistress seen here with me?

III   Whom *did* I marry?

IV   What ballet made my protégée a star?

40

THAT most famous of all Romantic ballet divertissements, Pas de Quatre *of 1845, was not without its share of backstage* Sturm und Drang. *Early that year, it was announced by Benjamin Lumley, manager of Her Majesty's Theatre, London, that Marie Taglioni, Fanny Cerrito, and Carlotta Grisi, the greatest ballerinas of their day, save Fanny Elssler, would appear together in the same ballet the next season. The* Times *didn't hesitate to predict that this meeting of artistic egos and temperaments would result in a "collision that the most carelessly managed railroad could hardly hope to equal." Jules Perrot, the brilliant dancer and ballet master, was engaged to stage the event soon after it was decided that Lucile Grahn, the young Danish ballerina who had just had a great success in London, would be included. After stormy negotiations at the outset, rehearsals proceeded calmly enough until shortly before the ballet's premiere. Cerrito and Grisi began to quarrel violently over who should dance the second-place solo after Taglioni, the acknowledged senior ballerina. In face of the screaming and carrying on, Perrot ran to Lumley's office for advice (and perhaps protection!). After some thought, Lumley offered a suggestion that would have been cheered by diplomats at the Congress of Vienna. The eldest ballerina after Taglioni would have the second place, and the other two would follow according to their ages. When Perrot announced the decision to the ladies, they started to laugh nervously and with some embarrassment, and suddenly became very eager for the* other *to have the coveted place they had been screaming over only a short time before! The* Pas de Quatre *was performed peacefully at Her Majesty's Theatre, on July 12, 1845, and was cheered as "the greatest Terpsichorean exhibition that ever was known in Europe." The order of the solos ran as follows: Grahn, the youngest; Grisi, less than a year older; Cerrito, two years older; and finally Taglioni, the reigning Queen of the Dance.*

THIS is a moment from what is perhaps the most famous of all Romantic ballets.

I   What is the title of the ballet?

II   In what act does this scene occur?

III   Who are the principal characters portrayed here?

IV   Can you name the seven pairs of famous interpreters shown here and on the following pages?

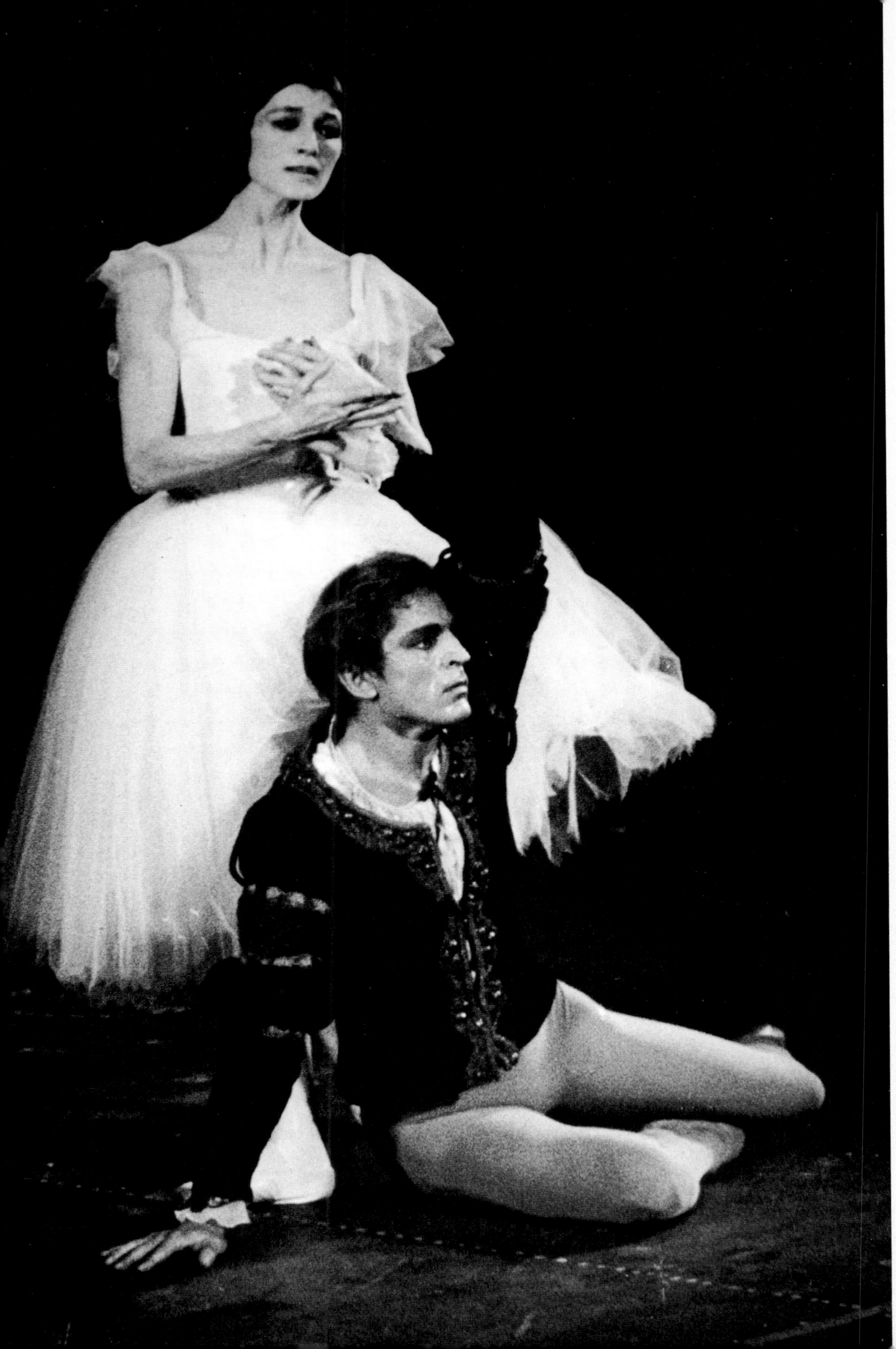

MARTHA SWOPE PHOTOS

[15]

THIS nineteenth-century print by J. Bouvier (opposite) shows an early cast of a ballet from which one of the most popular pas de deux in the contemporary repertoire is derived.

    I   What is the title of the ballet?

    II   Can you name these dancers?

    III   What famous ballet "team" introduced this ballet to the West?

    IV   What famous poet wrote the poem on which the ballet is based?

[16] WHO SAID IT?

"IN him is reincarnated the mysterious child Septentrion, who died dancing on the shore at Antibes. Young, erect, supple he walks only on the ball of the foot taking rapid, firm little steps, compact as a clenched fist, his neck long and massive as a Donatello, his slender torso contrasting with his overdeveloped thighs, he is like some young Florentine, vigorous, beyond anything human, and feline to a disquieting degree. He upsets all the laws of equilibrium, and seems constantly to be a figure painted on the ceiling; he reclines nonchalantly in midair, defies heaven in a thousand different ways, and his dancing is like some lovely poem written all in capitals."

Who wrote this, and what dancer was he describing?

[17] THE THREE GRACES

I What American writer wrote: "I should not say, of Taglioni, exactly that she dances, but that she laughs with her arms and legs. . . ."?

II Who wrote, about seeing Fanny Cerrito dance in *Le Pas des Déesses:* "It was something incomparably beautiful, it was a swallow-flight in dance, a sport of Psyche, a flight!"?

III Who wrote of Fanny Elssler, after seeing her in the ballet *Nathalie* in Boston: "The chief beauty is in the extreme grace of her movement, the variety and nature of her attitude, the winning fun and spirit of all her little coquetries, the beautiful erectness of her body, and the freedom and determination which she can so easily assume, and, what struck me much, the air of perfect sympathy with the house, and that mixture of deference and conscious superiority which puts her in perfect spirits and equality to her part."?

IV Can you identify which of these ballerinas is which in this print, "Three Graces" by A. E. Chalon?

[18]

THE full-length classics usually stress the importance of the principal ballerina role. But can you match these long-suffering ballet heroes with their rivals or nemeses and the ballets in which they appear?

1	James	A	Madge
2	Basil	B	Von Rothbart
3	Jean de Brienne	C	Carabosse
4	Albrecht	D	Madame Simone
5	Colin	E	Myrta
6	Franz	F	Gamache
7	Florimund	G	Coppélius
8	Siegfried	H	Abderakham

a *Coppélia*
b *Giselle*
c *La Fille Mal Gardée*
d *Swan Lake*
e *Sleeping Beauty*
f *La Sylphide*
g *Don Quixote*
h *Raymonda*

A

[19]

SEEN here and on the following pages are various interpretations in ballet of an exotic theme by Théophile Gautier.

    I   What is the title of the ballet?

    II   Who is the ballerina dancing the title role in (A), (B), and (C)?

    III   Who were the choreographers of (A) and (C)?

    IV   Who are the ballerinas' partners in (B) and (C)?

    V   What is the unusual fact about costume designs (D) and (E)?

    VI   What dancers were these costumes designed for?

55

[20]

THESE illustrations are from a famous ballet of the Maryinsky Imperial Ballet.

I   What is the title of the ballet?

II   Who choreographed it?

III   Who designed the set shown above?

IV   Who are the dancers in the principal roles shown opposite?

V   On what famous opening-night program was this ballet presented?

[21] FIREBIRDS

NAME the famous Firebirds shown here and on the following pages, the choreographers in whose productions they danced, and the companies with which they performed.

A

[22]

SEEN here are two costume designs from one of the great classics of twentieth-century ballet.

I What is the title of the ballet?

II Who designed the costumes?

III What are the names of the characters for whom they were designed?

IV Who were the originators of these two roles?

B

[23] PAVLOVA

  I When was Anna Pavlova born?

  II When did she graduate from the Imperial School of Ballet?

  III Who was her partner on her first tour outside Russia?

  IV In what year was that first tour?

  V In what year did Pavlova make her debuts in both New York and London?

  VI What was the name of her famous house and where was it?

  VII In what famous roles is Pavlova seen here?

  VIII What was the name of Pavlova's dog?

  IX Who was Pavlova's husband?

  X Where and when did Pavlova die?

PICTURED opposite is one of the most legendary of ballet's partnerships.

   I Who are they?

   II What is the title of the ballet they are dancing and who created it for them?

   III With what company were they most identified?

[25]

MATCH these classics of early ballet literature with their authors.

1	*Le Maître à Danser*	a	Bournonville
2	*Il Ballarino*	b	Feuillet
3	*Orchésographie*	c	Blasis
4	*Des Ballets Anciens et Modernes*	d	Arbeau
5	*Études Chorégraphiques*	e	Weaver
6	*Lettres sur la Danse et sur les Ballets*	f	Caroso
7	*The Code of Terpsichore*	g	Menestrier
8	*Neue und Curieuse Theatralische Tanzschule*	h	Rameau
9	*Chorégraphie ou l'Art de Décrire la Danse*	i	Noverre
10	*A History of Mimes and Pantomimes*	j	Lambranzi

THESE two designs are for one of the exotic ballets of the first part of the twentieth century.

    I   What is the title of the ballet?

    II   Who designed this ballet?

    III   Who was the choreographer?

    IV   When, where and by what company was it first performed?

    V   Who danced the principal female role?

    VI   Who wrote the famous score?

[28] NIJINSKY

I When and where was Nijinsky born?

II What was the profession of Nijinsky's parents?

III In what role at the Maryinsky Theater did Nijinsky cause a scandal that led to his resignation?

IV What was the first ballet Nijinsky choreographed?

V What was the maiden name of Nijinsky's wife? When and where did they marry?

VI What was their daughter's name?

VII Where was Nijinsky interned for a time during World War I?

VIII What was Nijinsky's last produced ballet? When and where was it presented?

IX Where did Nijinsky spend the duration of his long illness?

X When and where did Nijinsky die?

XI Where is he buried?

[29]

ON the following pages the immortal Nijinsky is shown in four roles created for him. What are they?

A

c

THESE four characters are from the first production (the choreography for which is now lost) of an early masterpiece of twentieth-century ballet.

   I   What is the title of the ballet?

   II   Who was its choreographer?

   III   Who wrote the score that caused a furor at its premiere?

   IV   When, where, and by what ballet company was this ballet given its premiere?

   V   Who designed this ballet?

[30]

This costume was designed for a now legendary ballet.

   I   What is the ballet?

   II   Who designed the costume?

   III   Who was the first dancer to wear it?

IN 1924, the Soviet State Dancers, a small group of young graduates from the Maryinsky Ballet School, were permitted by the Soviet Government to take their repertoire of "experimental" modern ballets on a limited tour of German health spas. Among the dancers were George Balanchivadze, the upstart choreographer, Tamara Gevergeva, his wife, and Alexandra Danilova, a brilliant young dancer with extra reserves of "spunk." The group danced the unconventional repertoire of Balanchivadze (soon to be renamed Balanchine by Diaghilev) with such success that their tour was extended to London and Paris. Serge Diaghilev, then at the height of his power as the leader of the vanguard company of the ballet world, saw the group, was impressed, and invited them to audition for the Ballets Russes. Acceptance into the company meant that the young dancers could remain in the West and dance a repertoire totally unavailable to them in the Soviet Union. It was obviously the chance of a lifetime. Geva and Balanchine danced for Diaghilev, who liked what he saw. Turning to Danilova, he said, "And so, what can you do, Danilova?" Being young and rather brash, the future prima ballerina of Diaghilev's company looked at the great impresario and said, "Meestair Diaghilev. Eef I am goode enough for Maryinsky Teeater, I am goode enough for you!"

BALLET dancers are required to dedicate so much of their time, concentration, and energy to their art, that they are rarely free to give much time to anything else. This total involvement in their own world has given rise to many negative remarks about the intellectual development and well-roundedness of dancers. Of course, nothing could be further from the truth; any person who can memorize sometimes as many as thirty different ballets, all to different scores, and dance them six out of seven days a week for months at a time, cannot be intellectually undeveloped! And how many university-trained people can say that they have lived every day of their lives surrounded by and performing to the works of the world's greatest composers, artists, choreographers, and, sometimes, writers (as librettists or inspirational sources); or danced in the greatest opera houses and theaters of Europe, the Soviet Union, and the United States; or performed for and been the guests of presidents, prime ministers, princes, kings and queens? Most members of our major ballet companies can say they have done all of these—quite a well-rounded life experience! Still, even in the dance world, there are many fond anecdotes concerning dancers' total immersion in their work.

One special favorite concerns the famous ballerina who looked absolutely ravishing and glamorous beyond her years. While on tour in the United States, she was approached by an eager and infatuated gentleman as she was eating in a restaurant. "Pardon me, mademoiselle," he said, "but I must tell you that you are absolutely ravishing." "Oh, thank you," she replied demurely, but more concerned with finishing her meal. "I think you dance divinely," he continued. "Oh, thank you, very much," she replied. "I think you're the world's greatest ballerina." "Oh, thank you, thank you." "I would be honored if I could pay for your lunch." "Oh, thank you, thank you very much." "Oh, the pleasure is mine, and, by the way," he said almost panting, "may I ask what you're doing tonight?" She looked up at him with her large, dark, beautiful eyes, fluttering her lashes, and said, "Swan Lake."

[31] WHO SAID IT?

I have been very astonished at the reception of *Les Noces* by several of the leading London critics. There seems to be some undercurrent of artistic politics in the business. I find in several of the criticisms to which I object, sneers of the "elite," and in one of them a puff of some competing show. Writing as an old-fashioned popular writer, not at all one of the highbrow set, I feel bound to bear my witness on the other side. I do not know of any other ballet so interesting, so amusing, so fresh or nearly so exciting as *Les Noces.* I want to see it again and again, and because I want to do so I protest against this conspiracy of wilful stupidity that may succeed in driving it out of the programme."

    I   What famous British writer felt compelled to write this in defense of *Les Noces?*

    II   Who choreographed the first production of *Les Noces?*

    III   Who designed the costumes seen above?

    IV   In what year and by what company was the ballet first performed?

    V   Who wrote the score?

HERE is a scene from a ballet based on a famous tale with a Spanish theme by Oscar Wilde.

I What is the title of the story and the ballet?

II Who choreographed the ballet, and where and when was it first performed?

III Who wrote the music for this ballet?

IV What famous American theater designer did the decor?

V Who starred in the title role?

[33] NAME THAT BALLET

A young man entertaining lady guests is ordered away from a large salon by his father, the Master of the House. But the father himself is drawn to the room and decides to enter it. Once there, he joins the ghostly revels taking place in the salon and ultimately dances himself to death. As his body is being carried away, his son stands alone, knowing that he will suffer the same fate.

I   What is the title of this ballet?

II   Who was the choreographer?

III In what year and by what company was the ballet first performed?

IV   Who headed the first cast?

V   What is the name of the master and his son?

[34]

NAME the founders of the following international ballet companies.

I   Ballets Suédois
II   Ballets des Champs-Élysées
III   Sadler's Wells Ballet
IV   Ballets: U.S.A.
V   Het Nationale Ballet
VI   National Ballet of Canada
VII   London Festival Ballet
VIII Netherlands Dance Theatre
IX   Bat-Dor Dance Company
X   Australian Ballet

85

[35]

THE set and costume designs seen here are for two different productions of the same ballet.

    I   What ballet is it?

    II   Who designed the set?

    III   What was the year of the production for which it was designed?

    IV   Who designed the costume?

    V   What was the year of the production for which it was designed?

86

[36]

FIND the famous ballerina in this photo of a 1935
production of *Giselle*.

Who is she?

[37] NAME THAT BALLET

THIS ballet is famous for its portrayal of the chic, sophisticated, and frivolous society of the 1920s. The central figure of the ballet is a rather frantic lady carrying a cigarette holder.

    I   What is the title of the ballet?

    II   Who is the choreographer?

    III   In what year and by what company was it first performed?

    IV   By what English title has this ballet been known?

    V   What is the name of the central figure of the ballet, and who was the first to dance the role?

[38]

MATCH the real names of these dancers with their "Russianized" names adopted for De Basil's Ballet Russe de Monte Carlo.

1	Brigitta Hartwig	A	Lubov Rostova
2	Betty Cuff	B	Lisa Serova
3	Prudence Hyman	C	Vera Zorina
4	Lucienne Kilberg	D	Vera Nelidova
5	Elizabeth Ruxton	E	Polina Strogova

[39] WHO AM I?

I was born in a boxcar as my Georgian parents were fleeing the Russian Revolution. We finally settled in Paris where I became one of the great Olga Preobrajenska's prize students. George Balanchine discovered me when I was not yet fourteen years old. He invited me to join his short-lived Les Ballets 1933 company and created two roles especially for me. I was one of three ballerinas nearly always publicized together in Colonel W. de Basil's Ballets Russes de Monte Carlo, where I was dubbed "the Black Pearl of Russian Ballet" for my dark, exotic beauty (see opposite). My career included not only guest appearances with ballet companies throughout Europe and America, but roles on the Broadway stage and in motion pictures as well.

    I   Who am I?

    II   What were the two ballets Balanchine created for me?

    III   In what Alfred Hitchcock film did I appear?

[40]

IDENTIFY the family relationship of each pair of dancers below.

    I   Michel Fokine and Léon Fokine

    II   Nicolai Beriosov and Svetlana Beriosova

    III   Vaslav Nijinsky and Bronislava Nijinska

    IV   Alicia Alonso and Alberto Alonso

    V   Serge Grigoriev and Tamara Grigorieva

    VI   Léonide Massine and Lorca Massine

[41] WHO AM I?

ALTHOUGH I was born in St. Petersburg, I helped pave the way for ballet in the United States. I was a product of the Maryinsky Imperial Ballet School, and appeared with the Maryinsky Ballet for several years until leaving it permanently to join Diaghilev's Ballets Russes. I had already traveled abroad as the partner of Mme. Pavlova, but I must say I took Paris by storm during my first Diaghilev season in that city when I danced the role you see me in here. I decided to stay in the United States after the company's second tour, and started my long career of dancing and choreographing for the Metropolitan Opera, the Chicago Civic Opera, and the San Francisco Opera. I finally settled in California to teach and even choreographed a few films in Hollywood, where I died in 1951. Contrary to popular belief, it was I who first choreographed a ballet which, in a later version by Mr. Balanchine, was hailed as a masterpiece. But, Mr. Balanchine always had a special flair with Mr. Stravinsky! Anyway, my version of Mr. Prokofieff's classic children's ballet was a great hit for Ballet Theatre in 1940.

    I   Who am I?

    II   What was the role in which I so impressed Parisian audiences?

    III   What ballet did Mr. Balanchine have a greater success with?

    v   What is the title of the ballet that was a hit with Ballet Theatre?

[42]

HERE is one of the great ballerinas of our time. Opposite and on the following pages she is shown in four of the many roles she danced in her career.

I   Who is this ballerina?

II   In what roles is she shown here?

III   With what two ballet companies was she primarily associated?

IV   Because of a certain characteristic, this ballerina was frequently linked during the first half of her career with two other ballerinas. Who were they?

THIS design could easily be a lithograph hanging in a modern art museum, but it is actually the set design for a ballet.

I What famous Spanish artist created the design?

II What ballet was it for?

III Who choreographed the ballet?

IV What company first performed the ballet? In what year?

THROUGHOUT the 1930s, Ruth Page pioneered in the creation of Americana ballets. Perhaps her masterpiece of that period, surely her most triumphant piece in that genre, was Frankie and Johnny, co-choreographed with Bentley Stone for the Chicago WPA in 1938. Based on the legendary ballad of the sympathetic prostitute and the man who "done her wrong," the ballet was racy, raunchy, and rowdy. So much so, that Chicagoans packed the house for the entire six-week run at the Great Northern Theater. Seven years later, in 1945, Serge Denham agreed to risk mounting Frankie and Johnny for the Ballet Russe de Monte Carlo, even though it was completely alien to the essentially traditional repertoire of that company. When the ballet finally came to the City Center Theater in New York City, its controversial subject matter and unconventional choreography caused a scandal that reached all the way to City Hall. Not even the rehearsal period had gone smoothly. The rehearsal pianist found the outstanding musical score so impossibly vulgar that she refused to play it. But the ballet master, who also knew a thing or two about music, took over and played the piano for all the rehearsals, simply because he loved the music and the ballet. His name was George Balanchine!

Despite all the brouhaha over the New York production, audiences loved Frankie and Johnny, and John Martin of the New York Times hailed it the "Best Ballet of 1945."

[44]

AMERICANS DANCE THE CLASSICS

I   Who was the first American Giselle? Who was her Albrecht?

II   Which company presented the first full-length *Sleeping Beauty* in America?

III   When and where was the first New York performance of *Coppélia?*

IV   Which choreographer mounted the first full-length *The Nutcracker* for an American company?

V   Who was the first twentieth-century American Lisette in *La Fille Mal Gardée?* When and with which company did she dance it?

[45]

A large part of the success of Americana ballets, which grew into a distinctive genre in the 1930s and 1940s, was due to the originality of the scores commissioned from American-born composers. Name the composers of the American ballets listed below.

I   *Fancy Free*

II   *Billy the Kid*

III   *Ghost Town*

IV   *Frankie and Johnny*

V   *Fall River Legend*

VI   *Filling Station*

[46] PARTNERS ON AND OFF–STAGE

MATCH these members of De Basil's Ballets Russes de Monte Carlo with their mates in marriage.

1	Jan Hoyer	A	Eugenia Delarova
2	Germain Sevastianov	B	Natalie Branitska
3	Serge Grigoriev	C	Irina Baronova
4	Léonide Massine	D	Olga Morosova
5	Colonel W. de Basil	E	Lubov Tchernicheva

[47]

MATCH these ballets created by Léonide Massine with the composers who wrote the scores, or whose music was adapted, for them (in the second column) and the artists who designed them (in the third column).

1	*Union Pacific*	A	Hector Berlioz
2	*Beach*	B	Nicholas Nabokov
3	*Symphonie Fantastique*	C	Jean Français
4	*Les Présages*	D	Georges Bizet
5	*Jeux d'Enfants*	E	P. I. Tchaikovsky

a	Joan Miró
b	Raoul Dufy
c	André Masson
d	Albert Johnson/Irene Sharaff
e	Christian Bérard

[48]

HERE are two costume designs for one of the earliest "Americana" ballets.

   I   What is the title of the ballet?

   II   What American artist, famous for his depiction of the Roaring Twenties, designed the costumes?

   III   Who choreographed the ballet?

   IV   What company first performed the ballet?

   V   Where and when was its first performance?

103

[49] WHO AM I?

I was born in Moscow in 1917 and by the time I was fifteen, I was dancing in Paris in the famous *Chauve Souris* revue. My teachers in Paris were Volinine, Preobrajenska, and Kschessinska; it was their training that prepared me to assume the title of "ballerina" in Colonel W. de Basil's Ballets Russes de Monte Carlo in 1932. Massine, Lichine, and Fokine all created roles for me (in fact, I am seen below as the Florentine Beauty in one of Fokine's ballets). For many years I appeared as guest artist with ballet companies in the United States and Europe. At present, I am living in semi-retirement in California, still teaching at the school I opened with my husband.

I   Who am I?

II   What is the title of the ballet I am seen in here?

III   What famous piece of concert music was used, with the composer's collaboration, for this ballet?

IV   Whom did I marry?

[50] WHO AM I?

I was born in Omaha, Nebraska, and began my ballet training when my family moved to Chicago. Through my teacher, Berenice Holmes, I was given an audition for Colonel W. de Basil's Ballets Russes de Monte Carlo and was accepted into the company even though I was only fourteen and a half years old. During my years there, I earned recognition in many ballets by Massine, Nijinska, and Lichine, most notably in *Francesca da Rimini* and *Prodigal Son.* Later on I moved to Ballet Theatre, where my career continued to flourish: Antony Tudor created a number of solo roles for me and I danced the Lilac Fairy in Anton Dolin's staging of *Princess Aurora.* My biggest success, however, came in two Broadway musicals: one was by Agnes De Mille; the other marked the Broadway debuts of one of our outstanding American choreographers, a great American composer, and two inimitable lyricists.

   I   Who am I?

  II   What role am I seen in here?

 III   Who choreographed this ballet?

 IV   What was the name of the show by Agnes De Mille?

  v   What choreographer made his Broadway debut with the musical I starred in?

 VI   What was the name of that show, and who were the composer and the lyricists?

[51]

THESE three sets were designed by the same artist for three landmark American ballets.

    I   Who is the designer?

   II   What are the titles of the ballets?

  III   Who choreographed these ballets?

  IV   In what years were these ballets premiered?

109

THE American modern dance developed in the first third of the twentieth century, primarily as a reaction to what was considered the sterile and unnatural dictates of the classical ballet. At the forefront of the pioneer movement, which until recent years remained strongly opposed to the ballet, was Martha Graham. Along with Doris Humphrey, Charles Weidman, and Helen Tamiris, Graham struggled to establish an identity and recognition for modern dance as an indigenous form of American art. One ally was John Martin, the New York Times dance critic and one of the most fervent champions of the modern dance cause. In a series of lectures at the New School for Social Research, Martin invited modern dance leaders to explain their art and their purpose to the public. At one of the seminars in 1931, the floor was opened to discussion after Graham had explained her famous theories of "contraction and release." Standing up from the audience, a balding, obviously irritated man with a heavy accent asked Miss Graham if she ever intended to develop "natural" movement in her form of "dance art." Equally agitated, Graham responded, but not to the questioner's satisfaction. He pressed her again for an answer; she hastened to reply. At the height of their confrontation, the man made a disdainful gesture that prompted Graham, now at the end of her patience, to blurt out, "Obviously, you don't know anything about movement!" Martin, seeing no end to this contretemps, stood and announced that the session really had to proceed. He thanked Mr. Fokine, and though Graham tried to patch things up with the revolutionary of early twentieth-century ballet, the rift between the two artists was opened wider than ever.

[52]

THIS is a tableau from the original production of a landmark Americana ballet.

   I   What ballet is it?

   II   What company first performed it?

   III   Where and when was that performance?

   IV   Who choreographed it?

   V   Who created the principal roles (i.e., the couple in the center of the photograph)?

[53]

A major figure in American ballet is seen here dancing an early solo in a rather avant-garde costume designed
for her by an artist who, though he designed several ballets,
is better known for his abstract designs and constructions
for the modern dance. Above is the artist's original sketch
of this dancer in costume.

I   Who is the dancer?

II Can you name the dance?

III Who is the designer?

[54]

WHO choreographed the ballets based on these famous works of American literature?

  I   *As I Lay Dying*
 II   *This Property Is Condemned*
III   *A Streetcar Named Desire*
 IV   *Winesburg, Ohio*
  V   *A Rose for Miss Emily*
 VI   *Annabel Lee*
VII   *Age of Anxiety*
VIII *The Bells*
 IX   *Spoon River Anthology*
  X   *Winterset*

[55] NAME THAT BALLET

THIS modern satire based on a mythical story takes place in a sleazy saloon. Three broken-down lady dancers, one with a fan, the second with hoops, the third with a boa, try to arouse a man working hard at getting himself dead drunk. None of the ladies manages to grab his interest, but to make their time worthwhile, they and a waiter rob him when he falls over a table in a stupor.

  I   What is the title of this ballet?

 II   Who choreographed it?

III   Who wrote the musical score?

 IV   In what year and by what company was it first performed?

  V   What American company later performed it, and who were the five principals in that cast?

ONE of the great masters of twentieth-century art designed this costume.

   I   Who is the artist?

   II   For what ballet did he design this costume?

   III   Who choreographed the ballet?

   IV   What dynamic twentieth-century composer wrote the music for this ballet? What is the name of the piece and how old was the composer when he wrote it?

   V   In what year and by what company was the ballet first performed?

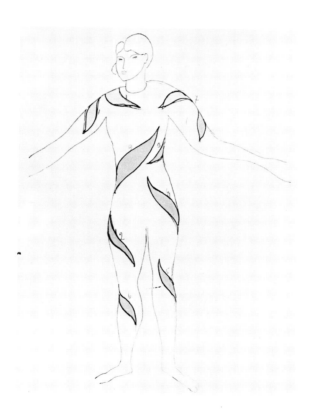

[57]

ONE of the most popular of all ballet partnerships
is seen above.

I Who are the famous ballerina and danseur
noble?

II What ballet are they dancing?

III With what company were they most
closely identified?

116

THIS moment is from one of the most joyful ballets in the contemporary repertoire.

I   What ballet is it?

II   Who was the choreographer?

III   Where, when, and by what company was it first performed?

IV   Whose music was used for the popular score?

[59] WHO AM I?

MY sister was acclaimed for her performances with the New York City Ballet and occasional seasons with American Ballet Theatre, but my career was far more varied. I danced with Ballet Theatre, the Original Ballet Russe, the Grand Ballet du Marquis de Cuevas, and was a guest ballerina with Ruth Page's Chicago Opera Ballet and the Harkness. Perhaps my greatest honor came in the late 1950s when I was named Première Danseuse Étoile of the Paris Opera, the first American ballerina to achieve that position. I now teach with my husband in Texas.

Who am I?

HURRELL, HOLLYWOOD

 [60]

THIS is a scene from a great dramatic ballet.

I   What is the title of the ballet?

II   Prominent in the photo are three of the original principal dancers of the ballet. Who are they? What roles did they dance?

III   Who choreographed the ballet?

IV   In what year was this ballet first performed?

THIS scene is from an American ballet that cata-
pulted its choreographer to fame.

    I What is the title of the ballet?

   II Name the members of the original cast
       seen here.

  III In what year and by what company was
       it first performed?

[62] NAME THAT BALLET

THERE is a church on one side of the stage and a cave on the other. One tricky character tries to get three others to enter the cave, from which they'll never return. Though the three victims give him a hard time, the canny trickster eventually triumphs.

I   What is the title of this ballet?

II   Who is the choreographer?

III   When was it first danced, and by what company?

IV   Who were the members of the first cast?

[63]

MANY ballets by the great twentieth-century choreographer George Balanchine are considered masterpieces and are now included in the repertoires of most major ballet companies throughout the world.

I   Can you name the dancers who headed the original American casts of the following Balanchine classics:

   (A)   *Apollo*
   (B)   *Serenade*
   (C)   *Concerto Barocco*
   (D)   *Ballet Imperial*
   (E)   *Theme and Variations*
   (F)   *Prodigal Son*

II   Who wrote the music for these ballets?

III   In what years and by what companies were these ballets first danced in the United States?

THIS unusual set was designed by a master of twentieth-century surrealist art.

I   Who is the artist?

II   What ballet is this design for?

III   Who was the choreographer?

IV   When and by what company was it first performed?

V   The choreographer and artist in question collaborated on another ballet best known for a finale that includes a "corps de ballet" of umbrellas. Can you name the ballet?

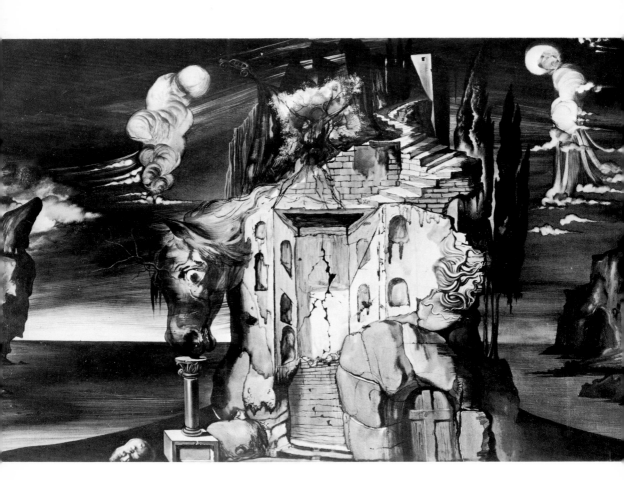

[65]

ABOVE is a scene from a ballet based on one of the most famous of Shakespeare's plays.

I   What is the title of the play and the ballet?

II   Who was the choreographer?

III When and by what company was it first performed?

IV Who designed the extraordinary set?

[66]

THIS arrested moment (opposite) is from the ballet _____.

    a *Apparitions*

    b *The Haunted Ballroom*

    c *Dim Lustre*

    d *Lilac Garden*

    e *Night Shadow*

Who are the principal couple in the foreground?

[67] NAME THAT BALLET

GUESTS gather in the garden of a French provincial farmhouse. Among them is a dejected young lady named Julia and her faithful companion dog, Pepe. The cause of her sadness, a young man in the company of his chosen lady, enters, followed by a group of attendants. A narrator wittily comments on these and other events that follow, until the day is over and Julia is left alone with Pepe, who vainly tries to cheer her up.

    I What is the title of this ballet?

    II Who choreographed it?

    III Who wrote the comic narration?

    IV On what other theater piece did this choreographer and writer collaborate?

    v Who first danced the role of Julia?

[68] BALLET STEPS

WHAT step is this dancer (opposite) executing with such effortless perfection?

Can you identify the dancer?

[69] PARTNERS ON AND OFF–STAGE

MATCH these dancers who are or were at one time married to each other.

1	Nana Gollner	A	Casimir Kokitch
2	Marjorie Tallchief	B	Herbert Ross
3	Alexandra Danilova	C	Paul Mejia
4	Nora Kaye	D	George Skibine
5	Cynthia Gregory	E	David Lichine
6	Diana Adams	F	Paul Petroff
7	Tatiana Riabouchinska	G	Terry Orr
8	Suzanne Farrell	H	Hugh Laing

THESE costume and set designs (opposite) are for a ballet based on one of the most famous short stories of a master American writer.

    I What is the title of the short story and the ballet?

    II Who is the writer?

    III Who designed the ballet?

    IV Who was the choreographer?

    V Who wrote the music?

    VI In what year and by which company was it first performed?

[71] NAME THAT BALLET

A young, unknown poet enters a hall where a lively masked ball is taking place. The Host introduces him to all the guests, including his favorite, The Coquette. After an entertaining divertissement, the guests leave the stage to the Poet and the Coquette, who dance together. The Host returns to claim the Coquette and the Poet is left alone onstage, until a moving light in the distance indicates the arrival of a beautiful but spectral woman. He dances with the deathly vision and his fate is sealed.

    I What is the title of the ballet?

    II Who choreographed it?

    III Who arranged the themes of what other composer for the score?

    IV When and by what company was the ballet first performed?

    V In the first performance, who danced the title role, the Poet, and the Coquette?

[72]

ONE of the great dramatic ballet partnerships of the forties and fifties is shown opposite.

    I   Who are they?

   II   What ballet are they dancing?

  III   With what ballet company were they most closely associated?

  IV   With what other company did they appear for a short time?

[73] NAME THAT BALLET

A young man from the city falls in love with a wild gypsy girl, who, for a short time, returns his love. When the girl decides to go off with a fellow gypsy, her rejected lover begs her to return, but to no avail. After a night of tormented dreams, the city youth murders the girl he loves and her new lover. His punishment is banishment from the gypsy tribe and a life filled with tortured memories.

    I   What is the name of the hero and the title of the ballet?

   II   Who choreographed the ballet?

  III   What is the name of the gypsy girl in this ballet?

  IV   Who created the three principal roles of the youth, the gypsy girl, and the gypsy lover?

   V   Can you name the poet upon whose work the ballet's libretto was based?

130

[74]

THIS is a scene from a very famous ballet film.

I   What is the title of the film?

II Can you name the three famous dancers
     seen here?

[75] MARGOT FONTEYN

I   When was Margot Fonteyn born?

II   Where did she study as a child?

III   In what ballet was Fonteyn's first leading role?

IV   What great comic role did she create in Ashton's *A Wedding Bouquet?*

V   When did Fonteyn first dance Aurora in *The Sleeping Beauty?*

VI   What was the first ballet created for her *outside* the Royal (then Sadler's Wells) Ballet? In what year?

VII   In what year was she created a Dame of the Order of the British Empire?

VIII   Whom did she marry and in what year?

IX   When did Fonteyn first dance with Rudolf Nureyev?

X   What ballet was created for Fonteyn by John Cranko?

[76] PARTNERS ON AND OFF–STAGE

THESE dancers (opposite), then husband and wife, made a sensation in New York when they danced in the ballet seen here.

I   Who are they?

II   What ballet are they seen in here?

III   When and with what company did they make their American debuts in this ballet?

IV   Who choreographed this ballet?

[77] WHO SAID IT?

"WHEN I was young I created ballets freely, spontaneously and without much thought; . . . Also, as befits the young, I wanted very much to please my audience and I thought it of great importance that I should entertain, amuse and charm them. Now I don't think that way. Up to a point I don't care what the audience thinks, I work purely and selfishly for myself and only do ballets which please me and which I feel will both develop me as an artist and extend the idiom of the dance."

Which of these choreographers said this?

a   George Balanchine
b   Jerome Robbins
c   Frederick Ashton
d   Antony Tudor
e   John Cranko

[78] ROMEO AND JULIET

THE story of Shakespeare's star-crossed lovers is one of ballet's favorite themes. Can you name the six Romeos and Juliets seen here and on the following pages, and the choreographers of the versions they are dancing?

[79]

MATCH the choreographers with their ballets based on stories of classical mythology.

1	*Medea*	A	George Balanchine
2	*Daphnis and Chloë*	B	Michel Fokine
3	*Orpheus*	C	Birgit Cullberg
4	*Icare*	D	Frederick Ashton
5	*Tiresias*	E	Serge Lifar

[80] NAME THAT BALLET

THIS ballet, originally known by its French title, is based on the story of the ill-fated romance of Tancred and Clorinda.

I   What is the title of the ballet? What is it in French?

II   Who choreographed this ballet?

III   What larger work of classic literature includes the story upon which the ballet is based?

IV   What American company first performed it?

V   What American ballerina received great acclaim for her portrayal of Clorinda?

[81]

CHOREOGRAPHER George Balanchine has used the waltz as the theme for several well-loved ballets.

I Can you name the composer of the music for each of the ballets listed below?

II In what years were they first performed?

    (A) *La Valse*

    (B) *Vienna Waltzes*

    (C) *Valse Fantaisie*
        (part of a larger work)

    (D) *Liebeslieder Walzer*

    (E) *Trois Valses Romantiques*

[82]

MANY Romantic ballets of the nineteenth century have fantastic plots; in the twentieth century, several major choreographers have dealt with the "fantastic" through abstraction, in ballets whose titles indicate the predominant mood of the piece.

I Name the choreographers of the "fantastic" ballets listed below.

II Can you name the composers whose music was used for each of these ballets?

    (A) *Scherzo Fantastique*

    (B) *Bourrée Fantasque*

    (C) *Irish Fantasy*

    (D) *Boutique Fantasque*

    (E) *Fantasies*

    (F) *Symphonie Fantastique*

142

[83]

GIVE the real names of these ballerinas:

    I   Melissa Hayden

    II   Margot Fonteyn

    III   Violette Verdy

    IV   Alicia Markova

    V   Allegra Kent

    VI   Suzanne Farrell

[84] NAME THAT BALLET

THE handsome Captain Belaye has every girlish heart in the town of Portsmouth aflutter. One especially determined young lady, the eponymous heroine of the ballet, decides to leave her devoted beau, Jasper, and join the crew of Belaye's ship, the *Hot Cross Bun*. She does not make a very good sailor and after some peculiar incidents, the ship returns to Portsmouth, where the discovery is made that all the crew were disguised ladies! There is a general reconciliation and happy finale.

    I   What is the title of this ballet?

    II   Who was its choreographer?

    III   Who wrote the music used for this ballet?

    IV   What series of ballads is the ballet based on and who wrote them?

    V   When and by what company was this ballet first performed?

    VI   Performances by what American ballet company made this ballet familiar to American audiences?

[85] BALLET STEPS

THIS position (opposite) is a common element in many classical pas de deux.

    I   What is the name of this position?

    II   Who is the ballerina executing it? Who is her partner?

[86] NAME THAT BALLET

A slave is in love with a Venetian courtesan. When he discovers that his mistresses, sisters of the courtesan's lover, plan to destroy the courtesan by thrusting arrows into a wax replica of her, he covers himself with a veil, assumes the place of the wax statue, and is stabbed to death by the jealous sisters, thereby saving his beloved.

    I   What is the title of this ballet?

    II   Can you name three of the four choreographers who have made versions of this ballet?

    III   Who wrote the beautiful score for this ballet?

    IV   Perhaps the most popular version of this ballet was performed throughout the mid-1960s. Whose version was this, and what company performed it?

    V   In this same version, who danced the title role?

[87]

THE boy shown opposite as the Nutcracker Prince in the New York City Ballet production of *The Nutcracker* went on to build a reputation as a great choreographic talent.

Who is he?

[88]

MATCH the choreographers with the ballets they based on biblical themes.

1	*After Eden*	A	Michel Fokine
2	*Prodigal Son*	B	Kenneth MacMillan
3	*David and Goliath*	C	John Butler
4	*Legend of Joseph*	D	Ninette de Valois
5	*Job*	E	Wayne Sleep
6	*Cain and Abel*	F	George Balanchine

[89]

THIS climactic pose is from the ballet ——————.

a   *A Birthday Offering*

b   *A Wedding Bouquet*

c   *Homage to the Queen*

d   *Gala Performance*

e   *Aurora's Wedding*

Can you identify the principal dancers in the foreground of this rare photograph?

THESE are two of a series of etchings by a great Spanish artist that inspired an American choreographer to make a powerful ballet. The pas de deux based on the etching at left, "If he were more gallant and less of a bore, she would come to life again," is one of the most memorable moments of the ballet.

I   What is the title of the ballet?

II   What is the name of the artist whose work inspired it?

III   In what year and by what company was it first performed?

IV   Who danced that famous pas de deux?

V   Who choreographed the ballet?

[91]

THESE designs (opposite) were created for a ballet first performed by the immediate precursor of one of the world's great ballet companies.

    i   What is the title of the ballet?

    ii Who was the designer?

    iii Who choreographed the ballet?

    iv For which company was it created and what was its premiere date?

    v Who danced the title role?

[92] NAME THAT BALLET

SOMEWHERE in an exotic forest, escaped convicts have built a fire in their camp to lure large butterflies. The convicts are joined by a recent escapee, who tries to capture the beautiful butterfly Morphide. The male butterfly Iphias sacrifices himself in the flames to enable Morphide to escape. As she does so, she marks the young convict with her golden pollen.

    i   What is the title of this ballet?

    ii Who is the choreographer?

    iii In what year and by what company was the ballet first performed?

    iv For what ballerina was this ballet created?

    v What does the title of this ballet mean in English?

THIS is a scene from a ballet based on one of the great realist plays of the late nineteenth century.

I   What is the title of the play and the ballet?

II   Who wrote the play?

III   Who choreographed the ballet?

IV   Can you name the dancers seen here in the principal roles?

V   What American ballet company has frequently revived this ballet?

VI   What American ballerina received some of her earliest public and critical acclaim in the title role of this ballet?

VII   Who was featured opposite her when she first performed it?

PICTURED opposite are the three principal characters in the original production of a ballet based on a famous work of French literature.

I What is the title of the ballet and the work it is based on?

II Who was its author?

III Who choreographed the ballet?

IV When and by what company was the ballet first performed?

V Who composed the music used for the ballet?

VI Who designed the ballet set and costumes seen here?

VII Who are the dancers who created the three principal roles, and what were the roles they portrayed?

THE DANCE COLLECTION (N.Y.P.L.)

THESE scenes are from two ballet versions of a great Shakespearean comedy.

    I   What is the title of the play?

    II   Who are the choreographers of these two ballets, and what are their versions called?

    III   Whose music is used for both ballets *and* in some productions of the play?

    IV   Who are the two famous ballet couples shown here? Name their roles.

SEEN here are two moments from one of the landmarks of twentieth-century ballet.

I   What is the ballet?

II   Who is the choreographer?

III   In what year was it first performed?

IV   What company first performed it?

V   Who created the leading roles?

VI   Can you identify the principal dancers in the photo opposite?

[97]

IN the picture above, a great American ballerina is making her solo debut.

    I   Who is the ballerina?

    II   What is the name of this role created for her?

    III   Who choreographed the ballet?

    IV   What is the title of the ballet?

    V   What was the year of its premiere?

    VI   Who was her partner in that performance?

MATCH these biographies or autobiographies with the ballerinas whose stories they tell.

1	*Bird of Fire*	A	Lydia Sokolova
2	*Dancing in Petersburg*	B	Tamara Karsavina
3	*. . . On Stage and Off*	C	Alicia Markova
4	*Theatre Street*	D	Maria Tallchief
5	*Giselle and I*	E	Mathilde Kschessinska
6	*Dancing for Diaghilev*	F	Melissa Hayden

FIND the famous ballerina in this photo of the Prologue from a production of *The Sleeping Beauty* in the early 1960s.

Who is she?

MYDTSKOV PHOTOS, COPENHAGEN

[100]

WHEN the Royal Danish Ballet gave their first
season at the New York State Theater, they performed a
ballet based on a Lap legend, scenes from which are shown
here.

    I What is the ballet?

   II Who choreographed the ballet?

 III What is the name of the dancer seen leap-
ing above?

 IV Who are the dancers at the right?

   v This ballet was in the repertoire of what
American ballet company for a time?

[101]

OPPOSITE is one of the century's most famous male dancers in one of the greatest male roles ever created.

    i Who is the dancer?

    ii What is the ballet?

    iii In what year was this ballet first performed?

    iv Who created this role?

    v In what year and with what company did the dancer pictured here first dance this role?

[102] WHO SAID IT?

"IT is frequently said that the costume should permit every possible movement of the body—an idea all the more dangerous as it is shared by many critics."

Which of these designers said this?

    a Isamu Noguchi

    b Kurt Seligman

    c Rouben Ter-Arutunian

    d Cecil Beaton

![decorative ornament] [103] PARTNERS ON AND OFF–STAGE

WHEN the careers of these two dancers (opposite) crossed paths, they not only danced together, they married as well.

ɪ   Who are they?

ɪɪ   In what ballet company did they dance together?

ɪɪɪ   With what other companies was she associated?

ɪᴠ   With what other companies was he associated?

ᴠ   What are their respective nationalities?

![decorative ornament] [104] WHO SAID IT?

"THE situation dictates form and method but not quality . . . It is true that in ballet you have freedom of choice in theme, in music, in style, in many things; but what I learned in ballet is to be found in . . . (my musicals), and what I learned in musicals is now found in my ballets."

Which of the choreographers said this?

a   George Balanchine
b   Jerome Robbins
c   Frederick Ashton
d   Antony Tudor
e   John Cranko

BELOW is a scene from a ballet based on yet another famous Shakespearean play.

I   What is the name of the play and the
ballet?

II   Who choreographed it?

III   When and by what company was it first
performed?

IV   Shown here are the dancers who created
the principal roles. Who are they?

[106] WHO SAID IT?

"NO piece of music, no dance can in itself be abstract. You hear a physical sound, humanly organized, performed by people, or see moving before you dancers of flesh and blood in a living relation to each other. What you hear and see is completely real. But the after-image that remains with the observer may have for him the quality of an abstraction."

Which of these choreographers said this?

a   George Balanchine
b   Jerome Robbins
c   Frederick Ashton
d   Antony Tudor
e   John Cranko

[107] NAME THAT BALLET

A modern allegory based on a poem by a famous French storyteller, this ballet concerns a young painter and his lover in a Paris garret. He longs to see the world, she only wants to stay at home. A passing gypsy caravan lures him away from his garret and mistress. After some unpleasant experiences with the gypsies, the painter returns home to his faithful love, and the couple are happily reunited.

I   What is the title of this ballet?

II   Who choreographed it?

III When and by what company was it first performed?

IV   Who danced the title roles?

V   What famous Frenchman wrote the original poem?

[108]

THESE scenes (opposite) are from two nineteenth-century classics performed by a company that took American audiences by storm during their premiere season in the United States.

    I   What is the company in question?

    II   In what year did they first visit the United States?

    III   Where did they first perform here?

    IV   What are the two ballets pictured here?

[109] WHO SAID IT?

"IT is true that the choreographer, the composer, the artist, every dancer, must know and have complete faith in the spirit of the work—and, for many, this is a kind of mystical knowledge, not reasoned understanding—but, because each of them is playing a particular part, he must concentrate on that part more than on the whole and unless this is so . . . the whole effect will be disturbed, perhaps even badly marred. Consequently the essential, motivating force must be supplied by somebody who is not a dancer, nor musician, nor artist, nor choreographer, but who has a mind sufficiently large and sufficient technical knowledge to embrace all these things."

Which of these designers said this?

    a Isamu Noguchi
    b Kurt Seligman
    c Rouben Ter-Arutunian
    d Cecil Beaton

170

THE scene shown opposite is from a ballet, based on a Japanese theme, that has been referred to by one critic as "hypnotically vulgar."

I   What is the ballet?

II   Who is the choreographer?

III   In what year was the ballet first performed?

IV   The visit of what company in what year inspired the choreographer to create this ballet?

V   Seen here are the original principal dancers in this ballet. Who are they?

[111] NAME THAT BALLET

THIS rather rollicking ballet consists of two vignettes. The first concerns a swarthy bandit captured by an Amazon Captain and her amorous band. The second involves a married lady of leisure who can't seem to decide which of her lovers she'll spend her leisure time with until her husband returns. The last scene is the triumph of Cupid, who manages to make some order out of chaos.

I   What is the title of this ballet?

II   Who choreographed the ballet?

III   What major non-New York-based company premiered the ballet?

IV   What New York company took it into its repertoire shortly thereafter?

V   Whose music is used for this ballet's score?

B

 [112] BALLET STEPS

TWO views of a ballet star at work.

I   Name the steps being executed so beautifully in (A) and (B).

II Who is the dancer executing them?

A

B

THE two ballets seen opposite have certain elements in common.

[113]

I   What are these common links?

II   What are the titles of these ballets?

III   When and by what company was ballet (A) first performed?

IV   When and by what company was ballet (B) first performed?

V   Who designed the costumes and decor for ballet (A)?

VI   Can you name the ballerinas who headed the casts of these ballets (seen here at the center of each photo)?

[114] NAME THAT BALLET

THIS modern three-act ballet with a historical background concerns a woman named Anna Anderson who claims to be someone else. Another of the roles is that of a great ballerina of the period in which the ballet takes place.

I   What is the title of the ballet?

II   Who choreographed it?

III   Who created the title role?

IV   What company first presented the ballet in a *one* act version?

V   What is the name of the ballerina in the first act of the full-length version, and who originated the role?

[115]

SEEN here is a costume design and a scene from a ballet considered to be one of the few truly successful modern comedy ballets.

   I   What is the ballet?

   II   Who was the choreographer?

   III   Who designed the costumes?

   IV   For what character was the costume on the left designed?

   v   The company that first performed this ballet was:

        a   American Ballet Theatre
        b   The Joffrey Ballet
        c   New York City Ballet
        d   The Harkness Ballet

179

IN the late 1960s, the Harkness Ballet performed several works that became almost synonymous with the company's name.

ɪ Can you name the choreographers of these ballets?

    (A) *Abyss*
    (B) *Canto Indio*
    (C) *After Eden*
    (D) *Monument for a Dead Boy*
    (E) *Time Out of Mind*

ɪɪ This is a scene from which of the ballets listed?

[117] NAME THAT BALLET

THIS ballet, which has been choreographed in different versions by major choreographers, tells the story of a child whose mother dies while attempting to protect him from the ravages of a snowstorm. Before the baby is rescued by local peasants, he is found and kissed by a dazzling white magical creature. Twenty years pass and the baby has grown into a young man about to be married. But during the pre-nuptial dance, the Bride is replaced by the mysterious white figure in disguise. Yearning after the symbol of his fate, the Groom goes off, deserting his unhappy would-be Bride.

I   What is the title of this ballet?

II   Who wrote the tale upon which it is based and what is the title of this story?

III   Who wrote the score for this ballet, and whose music is it based upon?

IV   Name the choreographers who have mounted versions of this ballet for:

    (A)   Ballets Ida Rubinstein
    (B)   Sadler's Wells Ballet
    (C)   American Ballet
    (D)   Royal Ballet
    (E)   American Ballet Theatre

PROPER *costuming for a ballet is always a major concern to a choreographer—it can completely alter the look of the choreographic design of a ballet, and even hinder its potential success. But, on the ballet stage, a work can usually survive the failure of its costumes. If the costumes are changed and the choreography revealed, the ballet may even have a great success and be hailed a masterpiece. George Balanchine's* Concerto Barocco *and* The Four Temperaments *are two cases in point. On the Broadway stage, however, every element of a ballet is crucial and the wrong costumes could easily contribute to the failure of the show. Balanchine was aware of this when he choreographed the Broadway musical* I Married an Angel, *starring his wife at that time, Vera Zorina. On opening night in New Haven, everything was in a state of crisis. It was obvious that the costumes for the surrealistic ballet Balanchine created for Zorina were all wrong. The ballet might fail. But what could be done now, at the last minute? Always calm, cool, and collected, Balanchine walked out the door, went to a store, bought twenty or so red, yellow, pink, and green* toothbrushes, *came back to the theatre, strung the brushes together and hung them around Zorina's neck. The ballerina went out on stage, and she, the ballet, the makeshift costume, and the show were all a success!*

182

THIS is a scene from a seldom-performed ballet
version of a classic nineteenth-century play.

    I   What is the title of the play and the ballet?

   II Who wrote the play?

  III Who choreographed the ballet?

  IV Whose famous music is used for this bal-
       let?

   V Can you name the ballerina soaring
      through this 1963 revival of the ballet by
      the London Festival Ballet?

A

THE two ballets seen here earned their young American choreographer great critical and popular acclaim.

I   What is the title of ballet (A)?

II In what year and by what company was it first performed?

III What is the title of ballet (B)?

IV In what year and by what company was it first performed?

V (B) is a photograph of the original cast. Can you name the dancers?

VI Who is the choreographer?

B

ONE of the great masters of twentieth-century art designed these costumes.

    ɪ   Who was he?

    ɪɪ   For what ballet did he make these designs?

    ɪɪɪ   Who choreographed the ballet?

    ɪᴠ   Who wrote the ballet's music?

    ᴠ   When and by what company was the ballet premiered?

    ᴠɪ   This production was revived by what American ballet company?

[121]

PICTURED above is one of ballet's most dynamic teams, in a ballet created especially for them.

I   Can you identify the dancers?

II   What is the title of the ballet and who created it for them?

III With which company were they most closely identified?

187

[122]

THE unforgettable music of Frédérick Chopin has been used for several major ballets.

    I   Can you name the choreographers of the ballets listed below?

    II   In what years and by what companies were they first danced?

        (A)   *Dances at a Gathering*

        (B)   *Les Sylphides*

        (C)   *A Month in the Country*

        (D)   *The Concert*

        (E)   *Constantia*

[123]

THIS happy group of dancers (opposite) includes the choreographer of one of the ballets in the previous Quiz as well as the cast from a production of that ballet mounted by the choreographer for a company other than his own.

    I   Who is the choreographer?

    II   What is the ballet?

    III   Can you name the dancers seen here?

    IV   When and with what ballet company did they dance this ballet?

[124] WHO AM I?

I was one of the most promising young dancers of the Royal Ballet; important roles were created for me by Sir Frederick Ashton and Kenneth MacMillan, though one of these was actually premiered by Rudolf Nureyev. I gave up my dancing career before I reached the age of thirty to pursue another career.

    I   Who am I?

    II   In what ballets were roles created for me by MacMillan and Ashton?

    III   Which of these roles was premiered by Rudolf Nureyev?

    IV   What career did I give up dancing to pursue?

    V   Can you name the ballet I am seen in at the right?

    VI   With what ballerina did I dance most frequently?

[125] WHO SAID IT?

"FOR ballet physical interference can be fatal, and need not even be discussed. Dancers have to move, and they must have space."

Which of these designers said this?

    a   Isamu Noguchi
    b   Kurt Seligman
    c   Rouben Ter-Arutunian
    d   Cecil Beaton

[126] BALLET STEPS

A famous star of the Bolshoi Ballet is seen, opposite, in action.

    ɪ   Who is he?

    ɪɪ   What step is he executing?

    ɪɪɪ   What role is he dancing?

[127]

THE profoundly moving music of Austrian composer Gustav Mahler has been used many times as the inspiration for choreographers.

    ɪ   Can you name the choreographers of the ballets listed below?

    ɪɪ   What are the German titles of the song cycles used for each?

        (A)   *At Midnight*
        (B)   *Dark Elegies*
        (C)   *Song of the Earth*
        (D)   *Song of the Wayfarer*

[128] WHO AM I?

I was born in Toronto, Canada, but my career as a dancer began and flourished in the United States. My first dancing assignment was with the Radio City Music Hall corps de ballet, but I soon joined Ballet Theatre, where I was immediately given solo roles. Antony Tudor gave me a new name, and it was with that name that I joined the New York City Ballet, my home for the next twenty years. During that time, I created many roles in ballets by George Balanchine, Jerome Robbins, and Frederick Ashton. As a parting gift, George Balanchine created one final ballet for me in my last season with the company. Also in that year, the City of New York bestowed upon me its highest cultural award.

   I   Who am I?

  II   What is the title of the ballet Balanchine created for me in the year I retired?

 III What year was that?

 IV What award did I receive from the City of New York?

[129]

CAN you name three American ballerinas in this photograph of *The Nutcracker* taken several years ago?

[130] CRITICS AND WRITERS

I Who was the first influential American dance critic (hint: he wrote for the New York *Times* in the 1910s)?

II For what newspaper did Walter Terry write for nearly thirty years?

III Who is Alexander Bland?

IV What British writer and bookseller was responsible for one of the most complete ballet chronologies ever assembled?

V Who was the founder of *The Dancing Times?*

VI Clive Barnes was associate editor of what British magazine before being appointed dance critic of the New York *Times?*

VII Who was the dance critic of the New York *Times* in the interim between John Martin and Clive Barnes?

VIII Who is the author of *Dancers, Buildings and People in the Streets?*

IX Who was the founder of *Dance News?*

X Who was co-editor of *Dance Encyclopedia* with Anatole Chujoy?

BEFORE 1948, The New York Public Library's material on the dance was meager, not to say nonexistant. Today, the Dance Collection at the Performing Arts Research Center, the New York Public Library at Lincoln Center, is recognized as the greatest archive of the dance in the world. The thousands of books, programs, librettos, clippings, photographs, manuscripts, posters, costume and set designs, lithographs and prints, scrapbooks, oral history tapes, the Asian Dance Archives and the millions of feet of film were acquired largely through the efforts of the indefatigable Genevieve Oswald, Curator of the Dance Collection from its inception to the present day. Her dynamic acquisition policies and inspired presentation of materials have made the Dance Collection a mecca for dancers, choreographers, designers, scholars, students, and the curious public in general. In the late 1940s, shortly after the Collection was established, Walter Terry, then critic for the New York Herald Tribune, decided to inverview Miss Oswald to find out what the Dance Collection was all about. After meeting the enthusiastic young lady and inspecting the few shelves and boxes that comprised the Collection, Terry asked, "But Miss Oswald, where is the Dance Collection?" "Why, Mr. Terry," she answered gaily, pointing to several recently acquired scrapbooks on her chair, "I'm sitting on it!"

ONE of the greatest partnerships of recent years is shown above in a classical ballet that brought them great critical acclaim.

    ɪ   Who are they?

    ɪɪ   What is the ballet they are dancing?

    ɪɪɪ   With what company were they most frequently associated?

[132] NUREYEV

I   What is the most unusual fact about Nureyev's birth?

II   When was he born?

III   Who was Nureyev's great teacher?

IV   When, where, and from what ballet company did Nureyev flee?

V   When was Nureyev's London debut? What ballet did he dance?

VI   When did Nureyev first dance with Margot Fonteyn? In what ballet did they dance?

VII   What ballet did Sir Frederick Ashton choreograph especially for Fonteyn and Nureyev? What year was it?

VIII   When, where, and in what ballet did Nureyev make his American stage debut? With whom did he dance? With what company?

IX   Nureyev has mounted his version of all of the following full-length ballets except one. Which is it?

a *Nutcracker;*   b *The Sleeping Beauty;*
c *Coppélia;* d *Raymonda;* e *Don Quixote*

X   Nureyev has danced with all of the following companies but one. Which is it?

a The Joffrey Ballet; b American Ballet Theatre;   c Murray Louis Company;
d New York City Ballet; e Martha Graham Company

SEEN opposite is one of ballet's great teams, dancing a ballet that is now almost synonymous with their
names.

    ɪ   Who are they?

    ɪɪ   What ballet are they dancing?

    ɪɪɪ   With what ballet company are they most
        closely associated?

[134] NAME THAT BALLET

THIS ballet, almost cinematic in scope, tells the
story of a slave, his love for his wife, and the slave revolt
he inspired, led, and ultimately died for.

    ɪ   What is the name of this hero and the
        ballet that bears his name?

    ɪɪ   What is the name of his wife in this bal-
        let?

    ɪɪɪ   What is the name of the Roman general?

    ɪᴠ   What choreographer's version created
        quite a sensation when it was brought
        to the United States in the late 1960s?

    ᴠ   What company performed this version?

    ᴠɪ   Who were the three principal dancers in
        that production?

    ᴠɪɪ   Who wrote the score for this ballet?

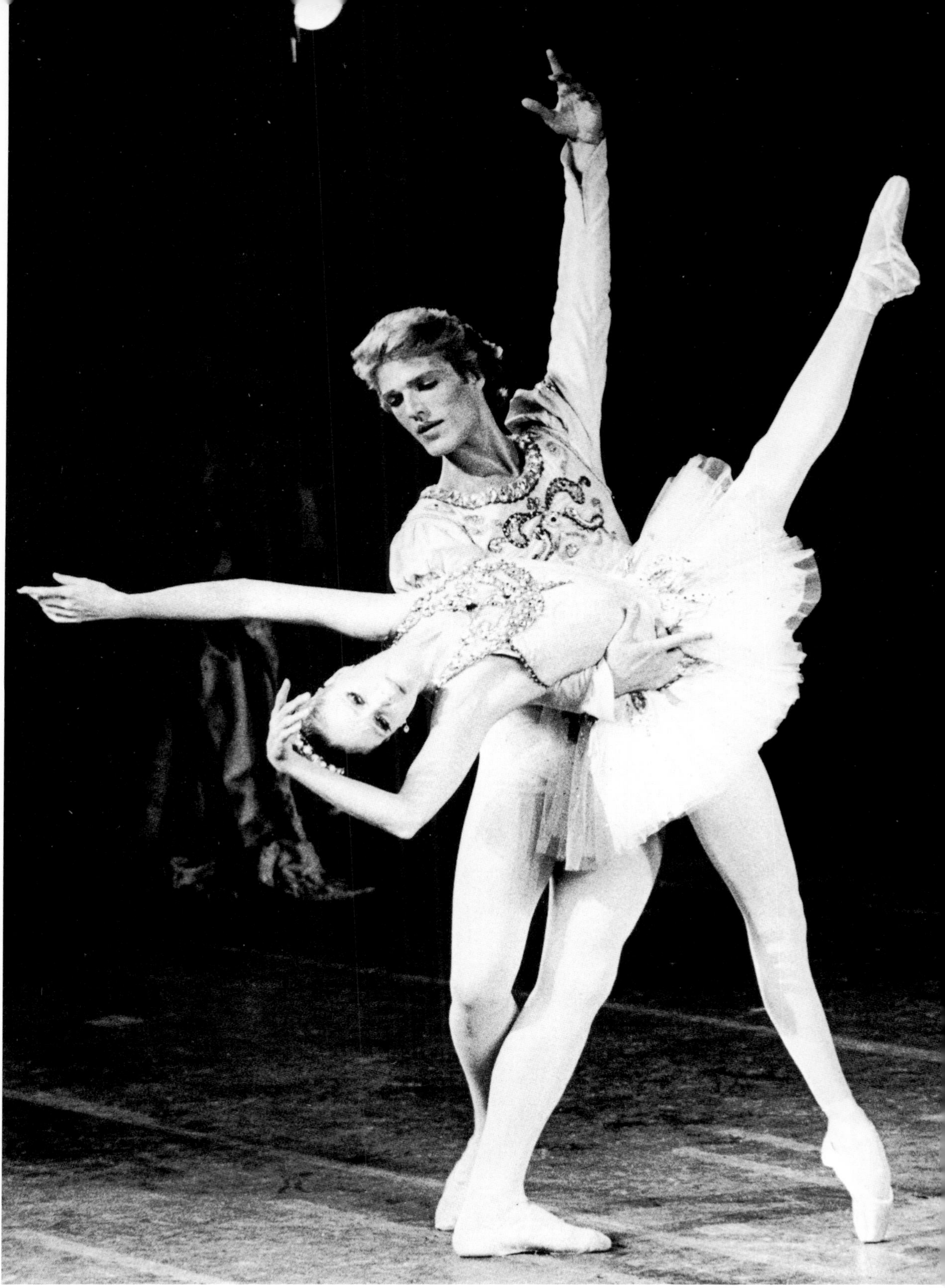

[135] PARTNERS ON AND OFF–STAGE

THE ballerina and premier danseur seen opposite not only dance together frequently, but are also married.

    I   Who are they?

    II   With what company are they associated?

    III   Where did he dance before joining his present home company?

[136] NAME THAT BALLET

STOPPING at the ruins of an ancient castle, the members of a 1916 motoring party are transformed into participants in the legend of Tristan and Iseult. After the story of the doomed illicit love is acted out, the action returns again to 1916. The motorists seem disturbed, but the cause of their malaise is unknown to them. They go off and leave the ruins to a mysterious caretaker who must have conjured the entire incident.

    I   What is the title of the ballet?

    II   Who was the choreographer?

    III   In what year and for what ballet company did he choreograph it?

    IV   Who created the roles of the Wife (Iseult), the Lover (Tristan), and the Husband (King Mark)?

    V   Who designed the scenery and costumes for this ballet?

[137] CYNTHIA GREGORY

I Where and when was Cynthia Gregory born?

II Who was her very great teacher before she became a professional dancer?

III With what company was she associated before joining American Ballet Theatre?

IV In what year did she join American Ballet Theatre?

V Name five ballets created for her in the repertoire of American Ballet Theatre.

VI In what year and where did she dance her now historic first performance of *Swan Lake?*

VII Name the ballet Gregory is seen in above. Who mounted this great classical ballet for her?

VIII In what year did Cynthia Gregory first "retire" (albeit temporarily) from American Ballet Theatre?

IX What particular honor did she win in that same year?

THIS is a scene from a ballet based on a famous fairy tale.

I What is the title of the tale and the ballet?

II Who wrote the story?

III Who choreographed this balletic version?

IV Can you name the dancers seen here in the principal roles?

[139] WHO SAID IT?

"IT does not matter what a ballet is about. So many people seem to think that the *subject* of a ballet, drama or painting is important. It is *how* it is, and what it is about that matters. It is the vision, the image, the metaphor of experience transmitted through legs and bodies."

Which of these choreographers said this?

a   George Balanchine
b   Jerome Robbins
c   Frederick Ashton
d   Antony Tudor
e   John Cranko

[140] NAME THAT BALLET

EQUALLY memorable for the wit of its choreography, its musical score, and the poetry which accompanied it, this ballet takes place in front of a Victorian setting. Two of the many highlights in the eight or so satirical vignettes are "Popular Song" and "Tango."

I   What is the title of this ballet?

II   Who choreographed it?

III Who wrote the musical score?

IV   Who wrote the poetry and recited it at the premiere?

V   What American ballet company recently took this British ballet into its repertoire?

A

B

HERE are scenes from two ballet versions of a great classic of Spanish literature.

I   What is the title of the book and the ballet?

II   Who wrote the book?

III   Who choreographed the version from which photos (A) and (B) were taken?

IV   The ballerina in (B) is dancing a principal role of that version. Who is she and what is the name of the character she is portraying?

V   Who choreographed version (C)?

VI   Who are the dancers seen here in the principal roles of that version and what are the names of the characters they are portraying?

AMONG the array of brilliant stars who have appeared over the decades with American Ballet Theatre, none stands above Natalia Makarova, the Russian-born ballerina who has dazzled audiences in the West, especially in America, for nearly a decade. It would be difficult to say which of Makarova's roles is most unforgettable, but a large portion of her enormous public would undoubtedly list her **Swan Lake** or her **Giselle** at the very top. The epitome of the prima ballerina, Miss Makarova is almost as well known for her performances offstage as on. During a recent ABT tour of the West Coast, Anthony Dowell, premier danseur noble of the British Royal Ballet and Makarova's partner for the tour, fell ill. In desperate need of a partner of equal stature, MaKarova turned to her compatriot, Rudolf Nureyev (then rehearsing with George Balanchine and Patricia McBride in New York) and requested that he fly to San Francisco to dance Siegfried at a moment's notice. Nureyev, with whom Makarova has had a rather shaky relationship over the years, dropped everything and rushed to her "aid"—a newsworthy event in the eyes of San Francisco's newspapermen. In the course of an interview with her, one of the journalists commented that a performance of **Swan Lake** featuring Makarova and Nureyev would be like a gala performance. She looked at the young man, and, with a grandeur worthy of a prima ballerina of pre-Revolutionary Russia, responded, "When Makarova dances, it is **always a gala performance!"**

213

The Answers

1   I (A) *Vestris* (B) *Medea* (with Carla Fracci) (C) *Hamlet Connotations* (with Marcia Haydée) (D) *Pas de Duke* (with Judith Jamison) (E) *Push Comes to Shove*

      II (A) Leonid Jacobson (B) John Butler (C) John Neumeier (D) Alvin Ailey (E) Twyla Tharp

2   Marie Camargo

3   I *tendu en avant*

      II Margot Fonteyn

4   (A) Charles Schultz's "Snoopy" (B) George Balanchine (C) Agnes De Mille (D) Théophile Gautier

5   I Gaetan Vestris

      II Auguste Vestris

6   c Louis Bouquet

7   I *La Sylphide*

      II Philippe Taglioni

      III 1832, in Paris, at the *Théâtre de l'Académie Royale de Musique*

      IV August Bournonville

      V (A) Marie Taglioni and Joseph Mazilier (B) Kirsten Simone and Henning Kronstam (C) Ghislaine Thesmar and Michael Denard (D) Gelsey Kirkland and Mikhail Baryshnikov

8   1 - D - b; 2 - E - a; 3 - A - e; 4 - C - d; 5 - B - c

9   1 - c; 2 - b; 3 - e; 4 - d; 5 - a

10   William Makepeace Thackeray

11   I Fanny Elssler

      II (A) *La Cachucha*

      III (B) *La Cracovienne* (C) *La Tarentule*

      IV The Park Theater

12   I Arthur Saint-Léon and Fanny Cerrito

      II He choreographed *Coppélia*

III *Lalla Rookh* by Jules Perrot, 1846

13 I Jules Joseph Perrot

II Carlotta Grisi

III Russian ballerina Capitoline Samovskaya

IV *Giselle*

14 I *Giselle*

II Act II

III Giselle and Albrecht

IV (A) Tamara Karsavina and Vaslav Nijinsky (B) Alicia Alonso and Ignor Youskevitch (C) Margot Fonteyn and Rudolf Nureyev (D) Alicia Markova and Anton Dolin (E) Carla Fracci and Erik Bruhn (F) Natalia Makarova and Ivan Nagy (G) Gelsey Kirkland and Mikhail Baryshnikov

15 I *Le Corsaire*

II Adèle Dumilâtre and M. Desplace

III Rudolf Nureyev and Margot Fonteyn

IV Lord Byron

16 Jean Cocteau, in *Commoedia Illustre,* 1911, about Vaslav Nijinsky

17 I Edgar Allan Poe

II Hans Christian Andersen

III Ralph Waldo Emerson

IV From left to right: Taglioni, Elssler, Cerrito

18 1 - A - f; 2 - F - g; 3 - H - h; 4 - E - b; 5 - D - c; 6 - G - a; 7 - C - e; 8 - B - d;

19 I *La Péri*

II (A) Carlotta Grisi (B) Anna Pavlova (C) Margot Fonteyn

III (A) Jean Coralli (C) Frederick Ashton

IV (B) Hubert Stowitts (C) Michael Somes

V The production for which they were designed (by Léon Bakst) was never produced by the man who

218

commissioned the ballet in the first place—Serge Diaghilev. The music was to have been by Paul Dukas and choreography by Fokine.

    vi   (D) Vaslav Nijinsky   (E) N. Trouhanova

20   i   *Le Pavillon d'Armide*

    ii   Michel Fokine, 1907

    iii   Alexandre Benois

    iv   Anna Pavlova and Vaslav Nijinsky

    v   At the opening night of the Ballets Russes de Diaghilev, Théâtre du Châtelet, Paris, May 19, 1909

21   (A) Tamara Karsavina; Fokine; Ballets Russes de Diaghilev

    (B) Alexandra Danilova; Fokine; Ballets Russes de Monte Carlo

    (C) Maria Tallchief; Balanchine; New York City Ballet

    (D) Maya Plisetskaya; S. Vlasov and N. Simachev, Bolshoi Ballet

    (E) Paolo Bortoluzzi; Béjart; Ballet of the Twentieth Century

22   i   *Petrouchka*

    ii   Alexandre Benois

    iii   (A) The Ballerina   (B) The Charlatan

    iv   (A) Tamara Karsavina   (B) Enrico Cecchetti

23   i   January 31, 1881

    ii   1899

    iii   Adolph Bolm

    iv   1907

    v   1910

    vi   Ivy House, London

    vii   (A) *The Dragonfly*   (B) *The Dying Swan*

    viii   Poppy

    ix   Victor Dandré

    x   The Hague, Holland, January 23, 1931

24 I Tamara Karsavina and Vaslav Nijinsky

    II *Le Spectre de la Rose,* by Michel Fokine

    III Les Ballets Russes de Diaghilev

25 1 - h;   2 - f,   3 - d;   4 - g;   5 - a;   6 - i;   7 - c;   8 - j;
    9 - b;   10 -e

26 I *Sheherazade*

    II Léon Bakst

    III Michel Fokine

    IV June 4, 1910, at the Théâtre National de l'Opéra, Paris,
    by Diaghilev's Ballets Russes

    V Ida Rubinstein as Zobeide

    VI Nicolai Rimsky-Korsakov

27 I December 17, 1889, in Kiev, Russia

    II Thomas and Eleanora Nikolaievna Nijinsky were
    dancers.

    III Albrecht in *Giselle*

    IV *L'Après-midi d'un Faun*

    V Romola de Putszky; September 10, 1913, in Buenos
    Aires

    VI Kyra Nijinska

    VII Budapest, Hungary

    VIII *Till Eulenspiegel,* in New York, 1916

    IX Switzerland

    X London, April 8, 1950

    IX Cimetière Montmartre, Paris

28 (A) The Golden Slave, in *Sheherezade* (B) *Petrouchka*
    (C) *Le Dieu Bleu* (D) The Faun, in *L'Après-midi d'un Faun*

29 I *Le Sacre du Printemps (The Rite of Spring)*

    II Vaslav Nijinsky

    III Igor Stravinsky

    IV May 29, 1913, in Paris, by Diaghilev's Ballets Russes

v   Nicholas Roerich

30   i   Nijinsky's *L'Après-midi d'un Faun*

    ii   Léon Bakst

    iii   Lydia Nelidova

31   i   H. G. Wells

    ii   Bronislava Nijinska

    iii   Nathalia Gontcharova

    iv   1923, by Diaghilev's Ballets Russes

    v   Igor Stravinsky

32   i   *The Birthday of the Infanta*

    ii   Adolph Bolm; at the Chicago Auditorium Theater, December 1919

    iii   John Alden Carpenter

    iv   Robert Edmond Jones

    v   Ruth Page

33   i   *The Haunted Ballroom*

    ii   Ninette de Valois

    iii   1934, the Vic-Wells Ballet

    iv   Alicia Markova, Robert Helpmann, William Chappell

    v   Tregennis

34   i   Rolf de Maré

    ii   Irène Lidova, Roland Petit, Janine Charrat

    iii   Ninette de Valois

    iv   Jerome Robbins

    v   Sonia Gaskell

    vi   Celia Franca

    vii   Julian Braunsweg, Anton Dolin, Alicia Markova

    viii   Benjamin Harkarvy

    ix   Bethsabee de Rothschild and Jeanette Ordman

    x   Peggy van Praagh

221

35   I   *Firebird*

      II   Nathalia Gontcharova

      III   1926

      IV   Léon Bakst

      V   1910

36   Margot Fonteyn is third from the right in the back row.

37   I   *Les Biches*

      II   Bronislava Nijinska

      III   1924, by Diaghilev's Ballets Russes

      IV   *The House Party*

      V   The Hostess; Vera Nemchinova

38   1 - C;   2 - D;   3 - E;   4 - A;   5 - B

39   I   Tamara Toumanova
      II   *La Concurrence* and *Cotillon*
      III   *Torn Curtain*

40   I   uncle/nephew

      II   father/daughter

      III   brother/sister

      IV   sister-in-law/brother-in-law

      V   father-in-law/daughter-in-law

      VI   father/son

41   I   Adolph Bolm

      II   The Chief Warrier in *Prince Igor*

      III   *Apollo*

      IV   *Peter and the Wolf*

42   I   Irina Baronova

      II   (A) Lady Gay in *Union Pacific* (B) Second Movement, *Choreartium* (C) Queen of Shemakhan, in *Coq d'Or* (D) Swanilda as Coppélia in *Coppélia*

III De Basil's Ballets Russes de Monte Carlo and Ballet Theatre

IV The other "baby ballerinas" were Tamara Toumanova and Tatiana Riabouchinska.

43 I Joan Miró

II *Jeux d'Enfants*

III Léonide Massine

IV De Basil's Ballets Russes de Monte Carlo, 1932

44 I Mary Ann Lee; George Washington Smith

II Catherine Littlefield's Philadelphia Ballet, 1937

III March 11, 1887, at the Metropolitan Opera House

IV William Christensen for the San Francisco Ballet, in 1944

V Lucia Chase, with the Mordkin Ballet, 1937

45 I Leonard Bernstein

II Aaron Copland

III Richard Rodgers

IV Jerome Moross

V Morton Gould

VI Virgil Thomson

46 1 - B; 2 - C; 3 - E; 4 - A; 5 - D

47 1 - B - d; 2 - C - b; 3 - A - e; 4 - E - c; 5 - D - a

48 I *Alma Mater*

II John Held, Jr.

III George Balanchine

IV American Ballet

V Adelphi Theater, New York City, March 1, 1935

49 I Tatiana Riabouchinska

II *Paganini*

III Rachmaninoff's *Rhapsody on a Theme of Paganini*

IV   David Lichine

50   I   Sono Osato

II   Rosaline in Tudor's *Romeo and Juliet*

III   Antony Tudor

IV   *One Touch of Venus*

V   Jerome Robbins

VI   *On the Town;* Leonard Bernstein, Betty Comden, and Adolph Green

51   I   Oliver Smith

II   (A) *Rodeo*   (B) *Fancy Free*   (C) *Fall River Legend*

III   (A) Agnes   de   Mille   (B) Jerome   Robbins   (C) Agnes De Mille

IV   (A) 1942   (B) 1944   (C) 1948

52   I   *Billy the Kid*

II   Ballet Caravan

III   Chicago, October 16, 1938

IV   Eugene Loring

V   Marie-Jeanne and Eugene Loring

53   I   Ruth Page

II   *Expanding Universe* (1932)

III   Isamu Noguchi

54   I   Valerie Bettis

II   Donald Saddler

III   Valerie Bettis

IV   Jeff Duncan

V   Agnes De Mille

VI   George Skibine

VII   Jerome Robbins

VIII   Ruth Page

IX   Donald Saddler

X   Stuart Sebastian

62   I *Three Virgins and a Devil*

      II Agnes De Mille

      III February 11, 1941, Ballet Theatre

      IV Agnes De Mille (the Priggish One), Lucia Chase (the Greedy One), Annabelle Lyon (the Lustful One), Eugene Loring (the Devil), and Jerome Robbins (the Youth)

63   I (A) Lew Christensen, Elise Reiman, Holly Howard, Daphne Vane
        (B) Kathryn Mullowney, Heidi Vossler, Charles Laskey
        (C) Marie-Jeanne, Mary Jane Shea, William Dollar
        (D) Marie-Jeanne, Gisella Caccialanza, William Dollar
        (E) Alicia Alonso, Igor Youskevitch
        (F) Jerome Robbins, Maria Tallchief

      II (A) Igor Stravinsky (B) P. I. Tchaikovsky (C) J. S. Bach (D) P. I. Tchaikovsky (E) P. I. Tchaikovsky (F) Serge Prokofieff

      III (A) 1937, American Ballet (B) 1934, Students of the School of American Ballet (C) 1940, American Ballet (D) 1941, American Ballet (E) 1947, Ballet Theatre (F) 1950, New York City Ballet

64   I Salvador Dali

      II *Mad Tristan*

      III Léonide Massine

      IV December 15, 1944, Ballet International

      V *Bacchanale*

65   I *Hamlet*

      II Robert Helpmann

      III May 19, 1942, the Sadler's Wells Ballet

      IV Leslie Hurry

66   c *Dim Lustre;* Hugh Laing and Nora Kaye

67   I *A Wedding Bouquet*

      II Frederick Ashton

III Gertrude Stein

IV *Four Saints in Three Acts*

V   Margot Fonteyn

68 A *cabriole;* Henning Kronstam

69 1 - F; 2 - D; 3 - A; 4 - B; 5 - G; 6 - H; 7 - E; 8 - C

70 I   *The Gift of the Magi*

    II O. Henry

    III Raoul Pène du Bois

    IV Simon Semenoff

    V   Lukas Foss

    VI 1945, Ballet Theatre

71 I   *La Sonnambula* (originally *Night Shadow*)

    II George Balanchine

    III Vittorio Rieti; Vicenzo Bellini

    IV February 27, 1946, the Ballet Russe de Monte Carlo

    V   Alexandra Danilova, Nicholas Magallanes, Maria Tallchief

72 I   Nora Kaye and Hugh Laing

    II *Lilac Garden (Jardin aux Lilas)* by Antony Tudor

    III Ballet Theatre

    IV New York City Ballet

73 I   *Aleko*

    II Léonide Massine

    III Zemphira

    IV George Skibine, Alicia Markova, Hugh Laing

    V   Alexander Pushkin *(Gypsies)*

74 I   *The Red Shoes*

    II Left to right: Robert Helpmann, Léonide Massine, Moira Shearer

75 I   May 18, 1919

    II   Shanghai, China

    III   Ashton's *Le Baiser de la Fée*

    IV   Julia

    V   February 2, 1939

    VI   Roland Petit's *Les Demoiselles de la Nuit,* in 1948

    VII   1956

    VIII   Dr. Roberto Arias, in 1955

    IX   February 21, 1962, in *Giselle*

    X   *Poème de l'Extase*

76   I   Nathalie Philippart and Jean Babilée

    II   *Le Jeune Homme et la Mort*

    III   April 9, 1951, Ballet Theatre

    IV   Roland Petit

77   c   Frederick Ashton, in "Notes on Choreography," from *The Dance Has Many Faces,* Walter Sorrell, ed. New York: Columbia University Press, 1966

78   (A) Alicia Markova and Hugh Laing, in Antony Tudor's version for the Ballet Theatre

    (B) Mona Vangsaae and Henning Kronstam, in Ashton's version for the Royal Danish Ballet

    (C) Marcia Haydée and Richard Cragun, in John Cranko's version for the Stuttgart Ballet

    (D) Lynn Seymour and Christopher Gable, in Kenneth MacMillan's version for the Royal Ballet, London

    (E) Galina Ulanova and Yuri Zhdanov, in Leonid Lavrovsky's version for the Bolshoi Ballet

    (F) Rebecca Wright and Kirk Peterson, in Ruth Page's version (from the television documentary, *Ruth Page: An American Original,* Otter Productions)

79   1 - C; 2 - B and D; 3 - A; 4 - E; 5 - D

80   I   *The Duel; Le Combat*

    II   William Dollar

III Tasso's *Jerusalem Delivered*

IV New York City Ballet

V Melissa Hayden

81 I (A) Maurice Ravel (B) Johann Strauss, Sr. and Jr., Franz Lehar, Richard Strauss (C) Mikhail Glinka (D) Johannes Brahms (E) Emmanuel Chabrier

    II (A) 1951 (B) 1977 (C) 1967 (D) 1960 (E) 1967

82 I (A) Jerome Robbins (B) George Balanchine (C) Jacques d'Amboise; (D) Léonide Massine (E) John Clifford (F) Léonide Massine

    II (A) Igor Stravinsky (B) Emmanuel Chabrier (C) Camille Saint-Saens; (D) Gioacchino Rossini (E) Ralph Vaughan Williams (F) Hector Berlioz

83 I Mildred Herman

    II Peggy Hookham

    III Nelly Guillerm

    IV Lillian Alice Marks

    V Iris Cohen

    VI Roberta Sue Ficker

84 I *Pineapple Poll*

    II John Cranko

    III Arthur Sullivan

    IV *Bab Ballads;* W. S. Gilbert

    V 1951, the Sadler's Wells Theatre Ballet

    VI City Center Joffrey Ballet

85 I *arabesque penché*

    II Svetlana Beriosova supported by Donald Macleary

86 I *Sebastian*

    II Edward Caton, Agnes De Mille, John Butler, Vincente Nebrada

    III Gian-Carlo Menotti

IV Butler's for the Harkness Ballet

V Lawrence Rhodes

87 Eliot Feld

88 1 - C; 2 - F; 3 - E; 4 - A; 5 - D; 6 - B

89 d *Gala Performance;* from left to right: Antony Tudor,
Miriam Golden, Alicia Alonso, Karen Conrad, Hugh Laing

90 I *Caprichos*

   II Francisco Goya

   III 1950, Ballet Theatre

   IV John Kriza and Ruth Ann Koesun

   V Herbert Ross

91 I *Orpheus*

   II Isamu Noguchi

   III George Balanchine

   IV Ballet Society, precursor of New York City Ballet,
   April 28, 1948

   V Nicholas Magallanes

92 I *Piège de Lumière*

   II John Taras

   III 1952, the Grand Ballet du Marquis de Cuevas

   IV Rosella Hightower

   V *The Trap of Light*

93 I *Miss Julie*

   II August Strindberg

   III Birgit Cullberg

   IV Kirsten Simone and Henning Kronstam

   V American Ballet Theatre

   VI Cynthia Gregory

   VII Erik Bruhn

94   I   *Illuminations*

        II   Arthur Rimbaud

        III Frederick Ashton

        IV March 2, 1950, the New York City Ballet

        V   Benjamin Britten

        VI Cecil Beaton

        VII Left to right: Tanaquil LeClercq (Sacred Love); Nicholas Magallanes (The Poet); Melissa Hayden (Profane Love)

95   I   *A Midsummer Night's Dream*

        II   (A) Frederick Ashton *(The Dream)*   (B) George Balanchine *(A Midsummer Night's Dream)*

        III Felix Mendelssohn

        IV Titania and Oberon are danced by (A) Antoinette Sibley and Anthony Dowell, and (B) Patricia McBride and Edward Villella

96   I   *Agon*

        II   George Balanchine

        III 1957

        IV New York City Ballet

        V   Diana Adams and Arthur Mitchell

        VI Allegra Kent and Bart Cook

97   I   Patricia McBride

        II   The Duchess of L'an L'ing

        III George Balanchine

        IV *The Figure in the Carpet*

        V   1960

        VI Nicholas Magallanes

98   1 - D; 2 - E; 3 - F; 4 - B; 5 - C; 6 - A

99   Natalia Makarova is the Fairy at the far left, in the Kirov Ballet production.

100 I *Moon Reindeer*

    II Birgit Cullberg

    III Niels Kehlet

    IV Henning Kronstam and Anna Laerkasen

    V American Ballet Theatre

101 I Edward Villella

    II *Prodigal Son*

    III 1929

    IV Serge Lifar

    V 1960, with the New York City Ballet

102 b Kurt Seligman, in "The Stage Image," from *The Dance Has Many Faces,* Walter Sorrell, ed. New York: Columbia University Press, 1966

103 I Marilyn Burr and Ivan Nagy

    II National Ballet, Washington, D.C.

    III London Festival Ballet; Hamburg State Opera Ballet; Australian Ballet (National Ballet Company)

    IV Budapest State Opera Ballet, New York City Ballet, American Ballet Theatre

    V Australian; Hungarian

104 b Jerome Robbins, in "New York is a Jerome Robbins Festival" (an interview with Walter Terry), The New York *Herald Tribune,* August 31, 1958.

105 I *The Taming of the Shrew*

    II John Cranko

    III March 16, 1969, the Stuttgart Ballet

    IV Marcia Haydée, as Kate, and Richard Cragun, as Petruchio

106 a George Balanchine, in "Marginal Notes on the Dance," from *The Dance Has Many Faces,* Walter Sorrell, ed. New York: Columbia University Press, 1966

107   I   *The Two Pigeons*

       II   Frederick Ashton

       III February 14, 1961, the Royal Ballet, London

       IV Lynn Seymour and Christopher Gable

       V   La Fontaine

108   I   The Leningrad Kirov Ballet

       II   1961

       III Metropolitan Opera House, New York City

       IV (A) *The Sleeping Beauty* (B) *Swan Lake*

109   d Cecil Beaton in "Designing for Ballet" (*Dance Index,* August 1946)

110   I   *Bugaku*

       II   George Balanchine

       III 1963

       IV Gagaku, the Musicians and Dancers of the Japanese Imperial Household, in 1959

       V   Edward Villella and Allegra Kent

111   I   *Con Amore*

       II   Lew Christensen

       III San Francisco Ballet

       IV New York City Ballet

       V   Rossini

112   I   (A) *sauté en arabesque* (B) *piqué arabesque* (first)

       II   Anthony Dowell

113   I   They are choreographed to the same music (Stravinsky's *Violin Concerto in D Major*), by the same choreographer, George Balanchine.

       II   (A) *Balustrade* (B) *Stravinsky Violin Concerto*

       III January 22, 1941, De Basil's Ballets Russes de Monte Carlo (then called Original Ballet Russe)

IV June 18, 1972, the New York City Ballet

V Pavel Tchelitchew

VI (A) Tamara Toumanova (B) Kay Mazzo

114 I *Anastasia*

II Kenneth MacMillan

III Lynn Seymour

IV Berlin Opera Ballet

V Mathilde Kschessinska; Antoinette Sibley

115 I *Souvenirs*

II Todd Bolender

III Rouben Ter-Arutunian

IV The Vamp

V c New York City Ballet

116 I (A) Stuart Hodes
(B) Brian Macdonald
(C) John Butler
(D) Rudi van Dantzig
(E) Brian Macdonald

II *Monument for a Dead Boy* (with Marlene Rizzo and War-ren Conover)

117 I *Le Baiser de la Fée*

II Hans Christian Andersen; *The Ice Maiden*

III Igor Stravinsky; P. I. Tchaikovsky

IV (A) Bronislava Nijinska (B) Frederick Ashton (C) George Balanchine (D) Kenneth MacMillan (E) John Neumeier

118 I *Peer Gynt*

II Henrik Ibsen

III Vaslav Orlikowsky

IV Edvard Grieg

V Marilyn Burr

   III Romeo in MacMillan's *Romeo and Juliet*

   IV Acting

   V Ashton's *Daphnis and Chloë*

   VI Lynn Seymour

125 c Rouben Ter-Arutunian, in "In Search of Design" *(Dance Perspectives 28)*

126 I Maris Liepa

   II *temps de poisson*

   III Crassus in *Spartacus*

127 I (A) Eliot Feld (B) Antony Tudor (C) Kenneth Macmillan (D) Maurice Béjart

   II (A) *Fünf Rückert Lieder* (only four of the five songs are used) (B) *Kindertotenlieder* (C) *Das Lied von der Erde* (D) *Lieder Eines Fahrenden Gesellen*

128 I Melissa Hayden

   II *Cortège Hongrois*

   III 1973

   IV The Handel Medallion

129 The trio in front of the Christmas tree are Suzanne Farrell, Karin Von Aroldingen, and Gelsey Kirkland (with doll), in George Balanchine's production for the New York City Ballet.

130 I Carl Van Vechten

   II The New York *Herald Tribune*

   III It is the pseudonym for collaborators Maude Lloyd and Nigel Gosling.

   IV Cyril W. Beaumont

   V P. J. S. Richardson

   VI *Dance and Dancers*

   VII Allen Hughes

   VIII Edwin Denby

   IX Anatole Chujoy

x   P. W. Manchester

131   i   Antoinette Sibley and Anthony Dowell

ii   *The Sleeping Beauty*

iii   The Royal Ballet, London

132   i   He was born on a train traveling between Lake Baikal and Irkutsk.

ii   March 17, 1938

iii   Alexander Pushkin

iv   June 17, 1961; Le Bourget Airport, Paris; The Kirov Ballet

v   November 2, 1961; *Poème Tragique,* a solo by Ashton

vi   February 21, 1962, in *Giselle* at Covent Garden, London

vii   *Marguerite and Armand,* 1963

viii   March 10, 1962, at the Brooklyn Academy of Music, in the *Don Quixote Pas de Deux,* with Sonia Arova, as guests with the Ruth Page Chicago Opera Ballet

ix   c   *Coppélia*

x   d   New York City Ballet

133   i   Suzanne Farrell and Peter Martins

ii   "Diamonds" from Balanchine's *Jewels*

iii   New York City Ballet

134   i   *Spartacus*

ii   Phrygia

iii   Crassus

iv   Yuri Grigorovich

v   the Bolshoi Ballet

vi   Vladimir Vasiliev (Spartacus), Ekaterina Maximova (Phrygia), and Maris Liepa (Crassus)

vii   Aram Khachaturian

135   i   Patricia McBride and Jean-Pierre Bonnefous

ii   New York City Ballet

iii   Paris Opera Ballet

136   I   *Picnic at Tintagel*

          II Frederick Ashton

         III 1952, the New York City Ballet

         IV Diana Adams, Jacques d'Amboise, and Francisco Moncion

          V Cecil Beaton

137   I   Los Angeles, California; July 8, 1946

          II Carmelita Maracci

         III San Francisco Ballet

         IV 1965

          V *The Eternal Idol* (Smuin); *Brahms Quintet* (Nahat); *At Midnight* (Feld); *Harbinger* (Feld); *Gartenfest* (Smuin); *The River* (Ailey)

         VI 1967, in San Francisco

       VII *Raymonda,* staged by Rudolf Nureyev

      VIII 1975

         IX The Dance Magazine Award

138   I   *The Steadfast Tin Soldier*

          II Hans Christian Andersen

         III George Balanchine

         IV Patricia McBride and Mikhail Baryshnikov

139   e   John Cranko, quoted in *Ballet in Camera,* Mike Davis. London: Oldbourne

140   I   *Façade*

          II Frederick Ashton

         III Sir William Walton

         IV Dame Edith Sitwell

          V The Joffrey Ballet

141   I   *Don Quixote*

          II Miguel Cervantes

Hausdorff
Compactifications